HIDDEN AXIS: FORCES BEYOND THE VISIBLE WORLD

SHEPARD AMBELLAS

ISBN: 979-8-9921959-0-3

Table of Contents

Part 2: Cosmic Forces and Ancient Prophecies

Part 3: Preparing for the Unseen

Part 4: The Coming Storm

Author Bio, Links, and Merch

PROLOGUE

The office was unremarkable. Stacks of files lined the walls, aging from yellowed documents to sleek, black binders marked with classified stamps and cryptic labels. The hum of a ceiling fan filled the silence, and the faint smell of stale coffee lingered in the air. On the desk lay a single document, its header marked by a bold insignia familiar only to those within the highest echelons of government. A casual observer might mistake it for an outdated file, but for those who knew better, it was a gateway to a hidden axis—a network beyond the visible world, where forces moved not to protect democracy, but to preserve power.

The file labeled Directive Alpha was more than an emergency protocol; it was a blueprint for the continuity of government—a system built to survive not only foreign attacks but also domestic unrest. Its purpose was to ensure the survival of authority and control, quietly set apart from public oversight. In this hidden axis, preserving the state meant protecting a carefully woven web of influence, a network designed to sustain itself even when the visible face of democracy was under threat.

For decades, this hidden network grew, embedded into the very foundation of government. Layers were added, security was tightened, and knowledge was kept strictly confidential, shared only with those who could keep secrets. In the event of a crisis, protocols could activate, unleashing a mechanism that would operate with quiet precision—a network designed to control, maintain, and protect its own existence.

It began as a Cold War contingency plan, a series of defenses against Soviet threats, nuclear fallout, and hostile foreign powers. But as time passed, this hidden axis adapted to new dangers, embracing the digital age. It evolved, integrating surveillance, real-time data collection, and covert alliances with technology firms to ensure that not only was the government protected, but that any force or faction posing a threat could be monitored, managed, and neutralized.

And then, in a single moment, contingency became reality.

September 11, 2001, was the day that activated these hidden forces, pulling them out from the shadows, if only briefly. As planes struck, and as Americans watched a city burn, the hidden axis that had been quietly maintained for decades roared to life. Clandestine protocols kicked in, whisking leaders to underground bunkers, silencing channels of communication, and mobilizing resources to enforce a lockdown on both information and movement.

In the years that followed, the American landscape transformed. Surveillance cameras became fixtures, satellites hovered above, and databases stored more information on individuals than they likely knew of themselves. For most, this was the price of security in a dangerous world. But beyond these visible systems lay an even more complex reality: a network where secrecy was its own currency, and where control became an unspoken mandate.

This book is an exploration of that hidden axis, a journey into the forces that shape our world from beyond the visible spectrum. It is a guide through the networks and mechanisms that hold the power to sustain—or subvert—democracy. It is an unmasking of the forces that prioritize control over transparency, the forces that continue to operate in silence, shaping society's future with every passing year.

In the pages that follow, we will peel back the layers of this unseen empire. From the Cold War paranoia that birthed these continuity programs to the AI-driven surveillance that watches us today, each step brings us closer to understanding the foundations of this hidden axis. It is a structure built for resilience, protected by secrecy, and concealed within the daily routines of a nation unaware of the forces that guide it.

This is *Hidden Axis: Forces Beyond the Visible World*. Welcome to the other side of freedom.

Part 1: The Foundations of Control

Chapter 1

Prelude To Secrecy: A History of Hidden Agendas

In the shadowy corridors of power, hidden from public view and the polished facade of politics, a clandestine structure exists—an unseen apparatus not designed for the American people but for maintaining control. Often referred to as the "deep state," this structure operates beyond public scrutiny, representing a murky authority built on decades of contingency plans, covert programs, and power preserved under national security. It is a structure that has endured wars, adapted to changing threats, and gradually entrenched itself deeper into the fabric of government with each passing decade.

The Birth of a Deep State Mindset

The origins of this hidden authority date back to the late 1940s, during a time when the world had settled into a Cold War marked by distrust and the looming threat of nuclear destruction. In post-World War II America, the rapid shift from being a wartime ally to an ideological adversary set the stage for a national obsession with preparedness and paranoia. For those in the highest levels of government, the possibility of a sudden, unprovoked attack on the United States was not merely hypothetical—it was a nightmarish scenario that demanded swift and decisive action.

At the core of this preparedness effort was a new governmental initiative known as the Continuity of Government (COG) program. Initially conceived as a response to fears of a Soviet attack, COG was established to ensure that essential government functions would continue to operate in a worst-case scenario. Leaders needed to feel confident that even if the unthinkable happened—such as a decapitation strike against U.S. leadership—there would be an intact structure prepared to carry on governance, make critical decisions, and maintain control.

Among the key figures shaping this mindset was Harry S. Truman. Despite assuming the presidency under sudden and tragic circumstances, he recognized the delicate balance of power that characterized the postwar era. Under Truman's leadership, the foundations of the modern security apparatus were established. The creation of the National Security Council (NSC), the Central Intelligence Agency (CIA), and the Department of Defense solidified a new governmental infrastructure focused on internal stability and external threats.

In this environment, secrecy evolved from merely a tactic into a culture—an essential requirement for preserving the integrity of a system that relied on the absence of public scrutiny. The term "national security" became a veil, concealing covert operations and internal directives under the guise of necessity. Those in power believed that the high stakes justified their means.

A Structure Built to Survive Anything

With the development of nuclear weapons, the threat of mutual destruction became a significant concern in global politics. This reality compelled the United States to rethink its approach to defense and survival, leading to the evolution of the Continuity of Government (COG) program into a layered and robust system. Nuclear fallout bunkers were constructed, emergency communication systems were installed, and evacuation plans were practiced—all under the oversight of agencies that expanded in size and scope without the knowledge or consent of the American public.

As the 1950s progressed, the COG expanded beyond Washington, D.C. In Virginia and Pennsylvania, in remote locations away from public scrutiny, government officials built secure safe havens known by codenames such as Raven Rock and Mount Weather. These locations became bunkers for critical leaders, complete with command centers, barracks, and provisions sufficient to last for months if necessary. They served as ultimate refuges—a place where the government could function in isolation, sheltered from the upheaval that might occur above ground.

This network of secure locations, protocols, and interagency cooperation established a foundation for a shadow system capable of replacing the official government in the event of catastrophic loss. The potential scenarios it prepared for expanded beyond nuclear war to include biological attacks, civil unrest, or even the collapse of the political structure from internal forces. The purpose of COG evolved to encompass more than simply protecting the government; it became about safeguarding those in power.

The Expansion of Emergency Powers

Throughout the 1960s and 1970s, as the Vietnam War and civil rights movements shook the nation, the role of the Continuity of Government (COG) program quietly expanded. With growing unrest and protests against the war, there was a perceived need for tighter control not just over external threats but also over the American public. National Guard troops were deployed domestically to respond to civil disturbances, and surveillance efforts began to target dissidents and activists.

The turning point came in the 1970s when social unrest reached its peak. Civil rights leaders and anti-war protesters were subjected to spying, infiltration, and, in some cases, neutralization by government agencies that justified these actions in the name of national security. The Federal Bureau of Investigation (FBI) and the Central Intelligence Agency (CIA) coordinated their efforts under programs like COINTELPRO, which aimed to dismantle political movements considered dangerous to the established order.

During this period, the COG program evolved into something beyond emergency preparedness. It transformed into a tool of control, an apparatus that could operate autonomously, wielding powers so extensive that even the president could be kept in the dark. The public needed to be made aware of the full scale of this system. When the Watergate scandal exposed corruption and abuse of power, revealing the concealed reach of intelligence agencies, the American people caught only a glimpse of what lay beneath the surface.

FEMA and the Formation of a Dual-Purpose Agency

In 1979, during the post-Watergate era—a time characterized by a widespread loss of trust in the government due to the Watergate scandal—President Jimmy Carter signed an executive order to establish the Federal Emergency Management Agency (FEMA). The agency's public role was straightforward: it was responsible for coordinating disaster relief and managing responses to natural disasters. However, another, less publicized mandate was equally crucial to the Continuity of Government (COG) structure. FEMA was intended to serve as a bridge between the civilian government and the military, enabling rapid deployment and centralized control in times of national crisis.

FEMA's responsibilities encompassed scenarios ranging from nuclear attacks to civil unrest. The agency's capacity for enforcing martial law and suspending constitutional rights during declared emergencies positioned it as a crucial component of the continuity program. Essentially, FEMA operated as a dual-purpose agency, capable of coordinating humanitarian aid or imposing military rule depending on the nature of the crisis.

For the American public, FEMA was viewed as a reassuring presence—a symbol of readiness and relief in the face of disaster. However, few understood the agency's shadow mandate or questioned the connections between FEMA, the Department of Defense, and various intelligence agencies. Behind closed doors, FEMA officials collaborated with military strategists to develop plans for situations that extended well beyond natural disasters.

Public perception of FEMA has primarily focused on its role as a disaster relief agency—a helpful yet often criticized force deployed during crises. Many remained unaware that its structure was designed to coordinate responses to hurricanes and earthquakes while also managing civil defense in the event of national unrest. FEMA's actual authority extends far beyond its public image, including powers that, under executive orders, could position it at the helm of martial law and national control.

This dual mandate was not a coincidence; it was part of a deliberate effort to create a civilian-military bridge that could be activated during significant instability. FEMA can deploy armed forces, restrict movement, and control communications during national emergencies. While these powers are often justified under the premise of protecting citizens, they also enable FEMA to sideline local governments, bypass traditional law enforcement, and enforce executive orders directly. FEMA operates as an extension of the deep state's continuity plans, wielding a substantial authority that becomes apparent only in severe circumstances.

The agency's evolution continued under the guidance of military strategists and intelligence analysts who recognized that a federal structure was crucial for maintaining order during nuclear, biological, or social crises. FEMA evolved beyond a disaster response agency to become an integral part of the continuity of government—a vital link between the federal government and military power. This transformation laid the groundwork for FEMA's gradual integration into COG operations, tightly connecting it to the nation's defense and intelligence sectors.

The Reagan Administration and the Deepening of Continuity Planning

The 1980s marked a transformative era for the Continuity of Government (COG) program, significantly influenced by the Reagan administration's assertive approach to national security. Convinced of an imminent threat from the Soviet Union, President Reagan and his advisors invested heavily in strengthening U.S. defenses, with COG being reframed as a crucial aspect of preparedness. During this time, continuity planning evolved from a passive safeguard into a more active and comprehensive system characterized by new directives, rehearsals, and the integration of continuity structures within various federal agencies.

One of the most significant actions taken during this period was the issuance of Presidential Directive 54 in 1984. This directive granted unprecedented authority to FEMA, the Department of Defense, and other agencies, enabling them to bypass the president and autonomously activate COG protocols in times of extreme crisis. Under this directive, these agencies could initiate continuity measures independently, with FEMA tasked with coordinating national control efforts if communication with top leadership compromised. As a result, FEMA was transformed from a civilian relief organization into a quasi-military entity capable of taking charge during national emergencies.

This reorganization led to numerous clandestine "readiness exercises" conducted under the direction of critical figures in the National Security Council, particularly Lieutenant Colonel Oliver North. These exercises, now well-known in the declassified records of the 1980s, simulated various scenarios ranging from Soviet nuclear attacks to widespread civil unrest within the United States. Civilian agencies and military units worked closely during these drills, testing plans for imposing martial law, relocating essential government officials, and controlling media communications.

Throughout these exercises, officials focused on preparing for external threats while assessing the potential for "internal disruptions." This broad term included civil disobedience, organized protests, and perceived threats from domestic opposition groups. The purpose of COG became increasingly expansive, indicating that these operations were intended to preserve the government during foreign attacks and manage domestic threats to stability. By the end of Reagan's second term, COG had evolved into a robust structure capable of managing crisis response independently and enforcing executive orders through FEMA when necessary.

The Rise of Surveillance: 1990s to Early 2000s

As technology advanced throughout the 1990s, so did the government's capacity to monitor, intercept, and analyze information. While physical safeguards like bunkers and secure communication lines had been the focus of earlier COG plans, sophisticated electronic surveillance opened a new frontier in continuity planning: information control. As digital communications became integral to modern life, intelligence agencies seized the opportunity to expand their reach, developing systems that allowed real-time tracking of data flows domestically and internationally.

One of this era's most notable surveillance initiatives was the Echelon program, a global surveillance network operated by the National Security Agency (NSA) in partnership with allies from the Five Eyes alliance, including the United Kingdom, Canada, Australia, and New Zealand. The program was initially created to monitor foreign communications, intercepting phone calls, faxes, and electronic messages. However, as Echelon grew, so did its reach, eventually capturing vast amounts of domestic data in addition to its international scope. Information collected by Echelon was compiled into databases, which could be accessed at a moment's notice by COG strategists and security officials, enabling them to react quickly to potential threats.

The digital age offered unprecedented insights into citizens' daily lives, and with the onset of the Internet, the NSA and other agencies expanded their surveillance infrastructure to match. The government began working with private telecommunications companies, allowing intelligence agencies to tap into data streams beyond traditional phone lines. By the late 1990s, monitoring capabilities had expanded to cover email, early web traffic, and emerging cellular networks.

This era also saw the development of databases and analytic tools designed to make sense of vast quantities of information. Known internally as data fusion, these tools allowed government agencies to sort, filter, and flag communications that matched specific keywords or patterns of behavior. The practical implications for continuity planning were profound: in a crisis, these systems could monitor dissident behavior, analyze population movements, and communicate directly with officials in charge of COG operations. Thus, surveillance technology became as essential to COG as secure facilities and transport, marking a shift from physical preparedness to information control.

9/11 and the Expansion of COG Authority

The attacks of September 11, 2001, signaled a new chapter for the Continuity of Government program. The sudden loss of thousands of lives and the vulnerability exposed on that day reaffirmed the need for an ironclad system capable of managing not only foreign threats but also domestic crises. Within hours of the attack, COG protocols were activated across federal agencies. Key officials were relocated to undisclosed secure sites, and FEMA and other emergency response agencies were placed on high alert as the country braced for further attacks.

In the months following the attack, Congress passed the USA PATRIOT Act, which expanded the surveillance capabilities of federal agencies, ostensibly to prevent future acts of terrorism. The act removed many of the legal barriers that had previously limited domestic intelligence gathering, enabling the FBI, NSA, and other agencies to monitor U.S. citizens more extensively than ever before. The passage of the Patriot Act effectively bridged the gap between COG's traditional focus on foreign threats and its growing interest in managing domestic risks.

New surveillance programs like PRISM and XKeyscore were launched following 9/11, allowing intelligence agencies to intercept data directly from major tech companies like Google, Facebook, and Apple. The programs collected vast amounts of electronic information, including emails, search histories, and even real-time chats, allowing COG strategists to monitor various online behaviors. Through these systems, the government gained the power to flag individuals based on their communication patterns, behaviors, or affiliations, positioning them for potential action under COG plans should they be deemed a threat.

As COG's digital reach expanded, so did its physical infrastructure. Secure locations like Mount Weather and Raven Rock were updated with state-of-the-art communication systems, underground command centers, and medical facilities to ensure that officials could operate without interruption in a crisis. Emergency drills and readiness exercises were conducted regularly, ensuring the continuity apparatus remained operational. The events of 9/11 transformed COG from a Cold War relic into a sophisticated, multifaceted system capable of managing nearly any conceivable disaster.

Modern-Day Implications: A Permanent State of Preparedness

Today, the Continuity of Government (COG) system is a silent but powerful presence within the American political structure. Over the decades, COG has evolved from a contingency plan for a nuclear attack into a vast network that spans multiple government agencies, private contractors, and technological infrastructure. An ever-growing list of threats, including international terrorism, cyber warfare, civil unrest, and global pandemics, has justified its expansion. Each new crisis has reinforced the government's commitment to maintaining control under any circumstances, solidifying COG as a permanent fixture.

The implications of this system are profound. The federal government has constructed a parallel structure capable of managing or bypassing traditional governance through FEMA, the NSA, and other agencies. Under the guise of readiness, the U.S. has embedded mechanisms for imposing martial law, restricting civil liberties, and overseeing the movements of its citizens—all in the name of continuity. COG has created a state of permanent preparedness that places unprecedented power in the hands of a select few, allowing them to take control whenever necessary.

Critics argue that COG's growth represents a dangerous shift toward authoritarianism and that the very powers intended to protect democracy can also be used to suppress it. The potential for abuse increases as each new surveillance tool is introduced and each emergency measure is codified. What began as a plan to safeguard against external threats now possesses the capacity to exert control over the American populace. The dual-purpose nature of FEMA and the expansion of agencies' surveillance powers suggest that COG has shifted from protecting the government to controlling its citizens.

In continuity planning, there is no endpoint, no "mission accomplished." The existence of COG implies that the government is constantly under threat and that this invisible structure can take charge at any moment. As technology advances, crises become more complex, and the line between security and control continues to blur, COG's role in American governance only deepens. The question remains not whether the government can survive a crisis but whether the American people will recognize their rights when it does.

The journey of Continuity of Government from a Cold War safeguard to a sophisticated apparatus of control is a testament to the complex relationship between security and liberty. The deep state has constructed an enduring framework designed to outlast any threat, evolving to encompass physical safeguards, surveillance, and information control. Today, COG's quiet presence within American governance serves as a reminder of the lengths to which power will go to ensure its survival.

As we delve deeper into the hidden mechanisms of control in the following chapters, we'll uncover the broader implications of a government that views its continuity as paramount, even at the expense of transparency and public oversight. The era of secrecy is far from over—if anything, it has only just begun.

Chapter 2

The Rise of the Deep State: An Invisible Empire

In the tumultuous years following World War II, as empires crumbled and ideological divisions emerged, the United States faced a new form of warfare characterized by secrecy and subversion. The U.S. and the Soviet Union, two superpowers in ideological opposition, recognized that military strength alone would not ensure dominance. Instead, they built intelligence networks, conducted covert operations, and developed contingency plans, establishing a silent foundation of power shrouded in mystery and intrigue.

As tensions rose, American officials realized that the visible branches of government—Congress, the judiciary, and the executive branch—were insufficient to defend the nation against evolving threats. Beneath the surface of democracy, a parallel structure was emerging, designed to safeguard the country and the interests of those in power. This "deep state" would influence American history, enduring political changes and growing stronger with each new crisis.

Post-War Foundations and the Creation of the CIA

As Cold War tensions escalated in 1947, the United States enacted the National Security Act. This significant legislation established the Central Intelligence Agency (CIA) and reorganized the military under a unified Department of Defense. The formation of the CIA marked the beginning of a new era for American intelligence, with the agency tasked primarily with countering Soviet influence abroad and, increasingly, within the United States.

The CIA quickly emerged as the central component of the U.S. intelligence framework, operating with limited transparency and civilian oversight. In its early years, the agency primarily concentrated on foreign intelligence and formed secret alliances with intelligence agencies throughout Europe and the Middle East. However, as the Cold War progressed, its operations became more ambitious. The CIA began conducting covert missions aimed at overthrowing governments, destabilizing opposition movements, and influencing global narratives.

One particularly controversial program was Operation Paperclip, a covert effort to bring former Nazi scientists to the U.S. after the war. Officially, the operation was intended to leverage German expertise in rocketry and other technologies. But among the scientists were experts in psychological warfare and espionage, men who had built their careers studying propaganda and psychological manipulation. Their knowledge found a home within the CIA, influencing the agency's approach to mind control, surveillance, and covert operations.

Through these programs, the deep state established a network designed to operate not only against foreign enemies but also in secrecy from the American public. This early period set patterns that would influence the following decades: compartmentalization, plausible deniability, and the capacity to bypass traditional checks and balances. What began as a temporary response to the Soviet threat quickly evolved into a permanent, invisible arm of the U.S. government.

Expansion of Power After the Kennedy Assassination

The 1963 assassination of President John F. Kennedy marked a pivotal moment for the deep state. Kennedy, a charismatic leader with a vision for America's role in the world, had grown increasingly skeptical of the CIA and other intelligence agencies. He was particularly wary of their covert operations, many of which by-passed executive oversight. Kennedy's desire to reduce U.S. involvement in Vietnam and his push to disman-tle portions of the intelligence community put him on a collision course with the very forces that had shaped post-war America.

After Kennedy's death, the deep state's influence surged, marking a significant turning point in its his-tory. Many within the intelligence community viewed his assassination as a necessary course correction, one that opened the door for more compliant leaders. Lyndon B. Johnson, Kennedy's successor, embraced a more aggressive stance in Vietnam and relied heavily on CIA intelligence to guide his policies. Johnson's alignment with the intelligence community set a precedent for subsequent presidencies, as the deep state subtly steered leaders to support its agenda.

From Richard Nixon's administration to the Reagan years, intelligence agencies leveraged their expanding authority to ensure that U.S. policy aligned with their objectives. Presidents who strayed from the deep state's agenda faced opposition and scandal, often driven by intelligence leaks and manufactured crises. With each new administration, the deep state grew more entrenched, embedding itself into the governance structure to the point where even the president's authority became secondary to its goals.

The Deep State's Strategic Pursuits and Operation Planet X

The dawn of the 21st century saw the deep state's focus shift toward a broader, more esoteric set of objectives. The collapse of the Soviet Union had diminished the Communist threat. Though terrorism and rogue states became the official enemies of the U.S., intelligence agencies pursued other matters behind closed doors. Among these clandestine operations was *Operation Planet X*, a covert mission conducted in Iraq in 2003.

Officially, *Operation Planet X* was part of the U.S. military's strategy to dismantle Saddam Hussein's regime, targeting Ba'ath Party members and suspected loyalists. However, beneath the public narrative lay a more profound mission. Intelligence operatives had long suspected that Iraq was home to ancient Sumerian artifacts that could hold secrets about historical cycles of catastrophe—ancient warnings etched into clay tablets and cylinder seals by a civilization that believed in celestial gods known as the Anunnaki.

U.S. forces raided sites throughout Iraq, obtaining not only military intelligence but also historical relics from ancient Sumerian sites. Among the items reportedly seized were Sumerian cylinder seals that described periodic planetary disturbances—events that the ancient Sumerians had attributed to the influence of the Anunnaki, beings they worshiped as gods who guided humanity's fate. These relics, once in the possession of the U.S. military, were classified, with their details hidden from the public.

This secret knowledge reinforced a growing belief within the deep state that the world faced a looming celestial event. As classified research into these artifacts progressed, intelligence reports began to suggest a correlation between these ancient predictions and the discovery of a mysterious celestial body known as Planet X, located beyond the known planets of our solar system. NASA's research indicated that this distant object might have a gravitational influence capable of destabilizing Earth's orbit, potentially triggering massive environmental upheavals.

To the deep state, these findings represented more than scientific curiosity. The prophecies of the Anunnaki and the discovery of Planet X validate the need for long-term continuity plans. Preparing for potential "biblical" catastrophes became an imperative—a mission not just to protect the government but to safeguard against a threat that, if accurate, could end civilization as we know it.

The Role of Black Budgets and the Military-Industrial Complex

As the deep state expanded in scope and ambition, its need for funding also grew. This funding sought to bypass traditional government oversight and operate without Congress or public scrutiny. The establishment of "black budgets" emerged as a solution to this problem, creating a pool of untraceable funds that could finance covert projects, undercover operations, and high-stakes missions like Operation Planet X. With these black budgets in place, the deep state was able to extend its reach even further, unencumbered by the constraints of transparency or accountability.

Black budgets became crucial during the Cold War when national security was a top priority. Agencies like the CIA, Pentagon, and NSA required funds for sensitive operations targeting the Soviet Union. These budgets were sourced from defense appropriations, funneled through layers of classified accounts, and obscured within general spending allocations. Over the years, these shadow funds became a permanent fixture in the federal budget, concealed in plain sight and shielded from external review. Billions of dollars flowed through these channels, financing everything from advanced weaponry to surveillance systems, with each new project contributing to the expansion of the deep state.

The military-industrial complex—an interconnected web of defense contractors, private intelligence firms, and technology companies—became the perfect partner for these initiatives. Major defense contractors like Lockheed Martin, Raytheon, and Northrop Grumman became pillars of this hidden economy, creating the tools and technologies that enabled the deep state to carry out its missions without detection. These corporations were not merely suppliers but partners, part of a vast machine of influence and control that blurred the line between public service and private profit.

Through these partnerships, the deep state's resources became virtually unlimited. Contractors developed cutting-edge surveillance technology, advanced weaponry, and data-processing systems, all fueled by funds invisible to both the American public and Congress. With each new development, the deep state strengthened its infrastructure, reinforcing its position within the government and society. The very existence of these budgets and their untraceable funds gave the deep state unprecedented power to act independently, setting the stage for the next phase of its agenda.

From Cold War to the Present—The Deep State's Modern Adaptations

The end of the Cold War in 1991 marked a significant turning point in global dynamics. With the collapse of the Soviet Union, which had long been considered America's primary adversary, the threat of Communist expansion diminished. For some, this was an opportunity to scale back America's intelligence operations and reassess the necessity of a vast and secretive power network. However, the deep state had different plans. It identified new threats on the horizon, rooted in political ideologies and tied to cosmic forces, environmental crises, and ancient prophecies that seemed to become more urgent with each passing decade.

Following the fall of the Soviet Union, the deep state shifted its focus. While official attention was directed toward terrorism, rogue states, and nuclear proliferation, a quieter concern emerged within intelligence circles: the potential for a global disaster caused not by human actions but by forces beyond Earth. The prophecies found in Sumerian artifacts acquired in Iraq and the discovery of Planet X hinted at an impending catastrophe of unprecedented scale that could surpass any human conflict.

After the events of September 11, 2001, the deep state found an ideal pretext to expand its power even further. The Patriot Act and new Homeland Security mandates provided vast authority to monitor and control civilian life. Surveillance programs like PRISM and XKeyscore were launched, allowing intelligence agencies to collect, analyze, and store vast amounts of electronic data. Though these systems were ostensibly designed to combat terrorism, they served a dual purpose, enabling the deep state to prepare for potential upheaval on a much larger scale.

As Planet X's trajectory and the Sumerian prophecies remained prominent, the deep state closely monitored individuals and Earth's environmental changes, tracking seismic activity, ocean currents, and atmospheric patterns. Under classified directives, NASA continued its research on Planet X, meticulously measuring its gravitational impact on the solar system. This data was integrated into deep-state operations, informing contingency plans encompassing everything from government continuity to large-scale population control measures.

By the early 21st century, the deep state had adapted its structure to operate on an unimaginable scale. Surveillance networks spanned the globe, data was harvested and processed in real time, and partnerships with private technology companies allowed unprecedented access to personal information. What had begun as a wartime measure evolved into a complex web of control, operating behind the scenes to address threats that the public could neither see nor understand.

The deep state now faced a more profound challenge: preparing for a potential cataclysm that, according to Sumerian legends, had previously destroyed entire civilizations. As this hidden network tightened its grip, it positioned itself to guide humanity through the coming storm, ready to implement measures to ensure its survival—regardless of the public's well-being. The rise of the deep state, evolving from a loose collection of post-war intelligence initiatives to a fully established shadow government, represented the culmination of decades of preparation. As time passed, its focus remained on current threats and the ominous possibilities ahead.

The rise of the deep state from the post-war shadows to an influential, unyielding network reveals a carefully cultivated architecture of control, built for survival and continuity above all else. With each crisis, each clandestine operation, and each technological advancement, this hidden axis strengthened, positioning itself as a guardian not just of the nation but of its own agenda. As we move forward, uncovering the layers of secrecy and purpose woven into the core of American governance, we confront a truth that has lingered in the periphery: the deep state is no longer just a contingency—it is a force shaping the world we live in, prepared to act in the face of forces beyond our understanding, and willing to rewrite the rules of democracy to ensure its own endurance.

Chapter 3

Operation Continuity: FEMA's Dual Purpose

The Federal Emergency Management Agency (FEMA) represents hope during disasters for many Americans. When hurricanes strike, wildfires rage or floods devastate communities, FEMA is the agency that promises stability, provides aid, coordinates relief, and assists in rebuilding efforts. However, beyond this compassionate image lies a different and more concealed purpose: FEMA is a significant and influential component of the Continuity of Government (COG) system, with responsibilities extending well beyond disaster relief. In the eyes of some, FEMA is not just a rescue operation; it is a critical part of a hidden network designed to ensure government survival at all costs.

When FEMA was established in 1979, its primary mandate was to assist during natural disasters. However, its foundational charter also included provisions for managing national security crises. Beneath its public-facing disaster relief mission, FEMA had directives for controlling resources, enforcing martial law, and coordinating with the military to maintain order during extreme situations. These hidden directives positioned FEMA as a support agency for continuity operations and an enforcer of the federal government's ultimate authority over the populace. Over the decades, this dual role has shaped FEMA into one of the deep state's most potent assets, prepared to mobilize quickly to enforce directives that most Americans would never suspect.

The Origins of FEMA and Its Public Mission

In 1979, President Jimmy Carter established FEMA as a civilian response agency focused on assisting Americans during crises. The agency was created to coordinate disaster response at the federal level, bridging the gap between local agencies and supplying essential resources to communities affected by natural disasters. The public understood FEMA's purpose to be clear: to be available when tragedy struck, ready to help Americans recover and rebuild.

FEMA's mandate has always extended beyond its humanitarian mission. Its foundational charter includes additional powers that allow FEMA to manage a variety of "national emergencies" under specific conditions. These emergency powers authorize FEMA to seize resources, restrict movement, and enforce curfews during crises. This dual role positions the agency as both a relief organization and an enforcement authority, prepared to mobilize and take control in situations where the continuity of government might be threatened.

Despite its extensive powers, FEMA's public image was carefully managed. Its involvement in natural disasters took center stage, leading most Americans to view FEMA as a benign agency focused solely on relief efforts. Over time, FEMA developed a reputation as a first responder, symbolizing the government's commitment to protecting its citizens. However, for those with insider knowledge, FEMA was more than just a disaster response agency; it was a foundational element of a broader network designed to maintain federal authority under any circumstances.

FEMA's Role in Continuity of Government (COG)

The hidden aspect of FEMA's mission reveals a more strategic purpose. FEMA was established to manage disasters and play a crucial role in the Continuity of Government (COG) network. This framework of systems and protocols is designed to ensure that the federal government can survive and function during any crisis. The COG network, developed during the Cold

War to prepare for nuclear conflict, includes various federal agencies and structures that maintain government authority even in catastrophic situations. FEMA is essential to this continuity network with its unique logistical capabilities and extensive emergency powers.

FEMA, as a crucial part of the Continuity of Government (COG), collaborates with military and intelligence agencies to prepare for scenarios that could threaten the stability of the United States. With its infrastructure and resources, FEMA bridges the gap between civilian governance and military control, allowing for the swift mobilization of federal forces and the coordination of state and local agencies. FEMA wields powers beyond its public image in this role, positioning itself as a vital enforcer within the continuity structure.

FEMA's integration into the COG network grants it sweeping authority in times of crisis. Under the COG framework, FEMA can mobilize resources, control public communications, and impose martial law if necessary. In the event of a nuclear attack, large-scale terror event, or widespread civil unrest, FEMA can activate protocols that suspend certain civil liberties, enabling it to enforce federal mandates without the checks and balances typically required in civilian governance. FEMA's ability to deploy these measures underscores its role as a significant force within the deep state—a tool designed to protect and maintain control.

FEMA has participated in numerous readiness exercises and emergency planning scenarios as part of its Continuity of Government (COG) responsibilities. These exercises often involve drills conducted alongside the Department of Defense and other federal agencies. Although these operations are mainly unknown to the public, they are designed to test FEMA's ability to respond to various crises, including nuclear fallout and large-scale natural disasters. During these simulations, FEMA's role was clear: to provide aid, secure critical government structures, and stabilize situations, even if it required imposing strict restrictions on the public.

Expansion of FEMA's Power Through Executive Orders

From the beginning, FEMA's authority was significant, but a series of executive orders has expanded the agency's powers even further over the years. These orders have positioned FEMA as a quasi-military force capable of taking control of essential systems during national emergencies. While the agency's primary role is to provide disaster relief, these enhanced powers allow FEMA to act as a powerful enforcer. This includes overriding local governments, controlling communications, and even restricting civilian movement under certain circumstances.

Among the executive orders that have expanded FEMA's authority are directives that grant it control over transportation, telecommunications, and public resources. Under these orders, FEMA can seize vehicles, reroute highways, and confiscate all means of transportation during a national crisis. Additionally, FEMA has authority over the national power grid and public communications systems, allowing it to manage information flow and energy distribution. In extreme situations, FEMA could restrict or shut down media channels and take control of broadcasting networks, ensuring that only government-approved information is disseminated to the public.

Beyond logistical control, FEMA's powers also extend to enforcing martial law. Specific executive orders allow FEMA to suspend constitutional rights, impose curfews, and deploy military assets within U.S. borders. In such a scenario, FEMA would operate as an arm of federal enforcement, working alongside military and intelligence agencies to maintain order. These powers, granted ostensibly to ensure continuity during catastrophic events, hint at FEMA's true purpose as a deep state tool, ready to secure government stability over public welfare.

Hurricane Helene provided a glimpse of FEMA's potential for exploitation. In the storm's aftermath, FEMA offered $750 "relief loans" to residents who lost homes or property. However, the fine print revealed a hidden catch: FEMA had the authority to seize their property if borrowers failed to repay the loans within a year. This tactic, mainly unknown to the public, underscored the agency's willingness to exploit disaster victims, positioning itself not as a benefactor but as a lender with the power to confiscate property. Furthermore, allegations surfaced that FEMA selectively provided aid based on political affiliations, bypassing homes displaying Trump campaign signs and sparking outrage among affected communities. These events revealed the agency's willingness to wield its authority selectively, leaving some to wonder if FEMA truly serves the people or a higher, hidden agenda.

Through its executive orders and discretionary powers, FEMA has become a formidable force, its actions obscured by bureaucracy and legal provisions. While the public sees an agency devoted to helping communities recover, FEMA's authority can transform it into a powerful enforcer in times of crisis. This duality—disaster relief on one hand and control on the other—has made FEMA a crucial element in the deep state's continuity strategy, prepared to assume sweeping authority in the name of national stability.

FEMA and COG Drills and Readiness Exercises

FEMA regularly participates in large-scale drills and continuity exercises to test its readiness to respond to various crises. These drills are conducted in coordination with the Department of Defense, the National Guard, and intelligence agencies, and they simulate a range of scenarios, from nuclear attacks to domestic unrest. Through these exercises, FEMA refines its role as an enforcer within the Continuity of Government (COG) network, preparing to mobilize at the national level should government stability ever be threatened.

One of the most notable drills was *Operation Garden Plot*, a federal plan to use military forces in response to large-scale civil disturbances. Initiated in the 1960s and updated regularly, *Operation Garden Plot* outlines procedures for handling riots, anti-war protests, and other forms of domestic unrest. FEMA's role in these exercises has been supporting military operations, coordinating resources, managing population control, and ensuring local governments comply with federal directives. In a full activation of *Operation Garden Plot*, FEMA could control entire regions, enforce curfews, limit movement, and oversee military personnel deployment in civilian areas.

Another significant exercise was *Rex 84* (Readiness Exercise 1984), a continuity drill that simulated the mass detention of American citizens during a national emergency. Originally designed as a response to potential waves of Central American immigrants, *Rex 84* tested FEMA's ability to establish detention camps, manage large-scale population movements, and enforce martial law. Critics of *Rex 84* saw it as a troubling example of FEMA's hidden purpose, suggesting that the agency's powers could be used not just to manage immigrants but to detain U.S. citizens in the event of civil unrest. While officially denied, documents obtained by investigative journalists indicated that *Rex 84* included scenarios involving the arrest of "subversive elements" within the U.S., raising questions about the agency's true preparedness mission.

The drills emphasize FEMA's evolution into a significant enforcer of continuity plans. During these exercises, FEMA's responsibilities extend beyond its primary public mission to include population control, resource management, and military coordination. The secrecy surrounding these drills highlights FEMA's role as a continuity enforcer, equipped to take decisive action in extreme situations, even at the potential cost of civil liberties. For those concerned about government overreach, FEMA's preparedness to mobilize during these operations reinforces its position as a crucial instrument for ensuring governmental stability—a force tasked with maintaining control and order, even if it means limiting the public's freedoms.

FEMA's Role in the Event of a Cosmic or Environmental Catastrophe

In addition to its domestic disaster response and continuity planning, FEMA has quietly prepared for scenarios involving extreme environmental and cosmic threats. As part of its mandate within the Continuity of Government (COG) framework, FEMA has developed protocols for handling events that could potentially devastate the nation on an unprecedented scale, including large-scale volcanic eruptions and asteroid impacts. Collaborating with agencies like NASA and NOAA, FEMA's role extends into monitoring, response, and population control measures that prioritize government stability over all else.

Preparing for Volcanic Eruptions

One significant environmental threat FEMA has prepared for is the possibility of a massive volcanic eruption. In particular, the agency has focused on monitoring supervolcano sites within the United States, such as Yellowstone. A major eruption from a supervolcano could eject thousands of cubic kilometers of ash into the atmosphere, blocking sunlight and triggering a volcanic winter that would drastically alter global climates. Such an event could lead to mass crop failures, severe disruptions to transportation, and health risks from inhaled ash.

In collaboration with the U.S. Geological Survey (USGS), FEMA has developed response plans, including mass evacuations, establishment of exclusion zones, and coordination with the National Guard to maintain order in affected areas. Additionally, FEMA's contingency plans outline provisions for distributing food and medical supplies to mitigate the impacts of a volcanic winter. However, in extreme scenarios, these plans also empower FEMA to impose curfews, control movement, and take control of resources. If a supervolcano were to erupt, FEMA's priority would shift from aiding the public to maintaining government continuity and social stability, even if it meant using military force to enforce compliance.

Contingency Plans for Asteroid Impacts

Another area where FEMA's role in cosmic event preparation has expanded is the threat of asteroid impacts. Through partnerships with NASA's Planetary Defense Coordination Office (PDCO), FEMA has monitored near-Earth objects (NEOs) that pose a potential impact risk. While the likelihood of a giant asteroid striking Earth is low, the consequences of such an event would be catastrophic, with impacts ranging from localized destruction to global climate shifts. An asteroid impact could result in fires, shockwaves, and massive tsunamis, creating a crisis requiring immediate and large-scale government intervention.

FEMA's asteroid impact response plan includes early warning systems, coordinated evacuation strategies, and population management protocols. In a credible impact threat, FEMA can mobilize resources, control transportation systems, and establish temporary shelters for those in affected areas. If necessary, FEMA can activate martial law, using federal and local military forces to enforce evacuation orders and maintain order. Though seldom discussed publicly, these preparations illustrate FEMA's readiness to handle scenarios beyond natural disasters, positioning it as a critical player in the government's continuity strategy.

Population Management and Martial Law

FEMA's plans emphasize maintaining control over the civilian population in scenarios involving either volcanic eruptions or asteroid impacts. FEMA's mandate includes managing evacuations, tributing supplies, and implementing martial law if necessary to prevent chaos and ensure government stability. Under these plans, FEMA can enforce strict population management, establish controlled zones, and restrict civilian movement. Military forces would assist FEMA in enforcing curfews, detaining those who defy orders, and securing critical resources for government use.

The contingency plans for these large-scale catastrophes reveal FEMA's dual nature. While it positions itself as a provider of aid, FEMA's proper role in the event of a cosmic or environmental disaster would be to uphold federal authority and ensure that government functions remain intact. In this scenario, FEMA's priorities align closely with the deep state's continuity agenda, ready to control the populace and enforce order, even at the expense of individual freedoms.

FEMA's Hidden Role in National Security

While FEMA's public image revolves around disaster relief and assistance, the agency's operations reveal a far more complex purpose. FEMA is not merely a support agency for disaster response; it is a powerful arm of the Continuity of Government (COG) and the deep state—a hidden apparatus positioned to maintain control in times of extreme crisis. Through its sweeping powers, FEMA has the authority to exploit vulnerable citizens, enforce selective aid based on ideological factors, and mobilize military resources, all while projecting a humanitarian facade.

As a critical player in the deep state's network, FEMA is primed for a role that goes beyond protecting citizens. In an unprecedented crisis, FEMA's ultimate mandate may be to protect the government itself, even at the expense of civil liberties, individual freedoms, and the Constitution. Ultimately, FEMA is an enforcer designed to support the deep state's continuity agenda, no matter the cost. The agency's extensive powers, secrecy, and influence suggest its purpose is not solely benevolent. Instead, FEMA is a critical tool in a larger plan that may one day be used for purposes far from what the American people would expect—or accept.

Chapter 4

Hidden Axis of Control: Surveillance, AI, and the Nanny State

In our contemporary world, the ubiquity of security cameras, the extensive storage of personal data, and the predictive capabilities of artificial intelligence have not just blurred the line between protection and surveillance, but have permeated every aspect of our lives. Beyond the visible oversight of the state, a more insidious and complex network of observation is at play. Bird-like drones, micro-insect spy devices, cameras embedded in self-driving cars, and robotic 'eyes' are not just technological marvels; they are integral components of a vast and expanding system dedicated to gathering intelligence on every facet of daily life. These tools, armed with military-grade artificial intelligence and supported by deep-state strategies, form a hidden axis of control that is increasingly encroaching on our privacy and freedom.

For the average citizen, modern surveillance is the price of safety in an increasingly unpredictable world. However, beneath this surface lies a crucial question of power: Who controls these eyes in the sky, these robotic observers, and these data-collecting vehicles, and why? As we delve deeper into this issue, it becomes increasingly clear that these tools are not just protective; they are part of an ecosystem that quietly erodes our freedom, continuously gathers data, and makes privacy an increasingly rare and precious commodity. The loss of privacy is not just a theoretical concept but a real and present concern in our daily lives, a concern that we must address.

The Evolution of Surveillance in the Digital Age

Surveillance technology has advanced significantly over the past few decades, particularly after September 11, 2001. This day marked a crucial turning point in the United States, prompting the government to seek new methods for identifying and preventing potential threats. In response, Congress passed the Patriot Act, granting intelligence agencies unprecedented powers to monitor personal communications, track individuals' locations, and collect extensive data on citizens and foreign nationals. However, the real game-changer has been the integration of advanced artificial intelligence into these surveillance systems. Although these tools were initially intended for counter-terrorism efforts, their scope quickly expanded. As a result, we now live in a digital landscape where surveillance, powered by AI, is widespread and often unavoidable.

Surveillance has evolved beyond traditional methods such as cameras and wiretaps. Agencies now deploy bird-like drones and insect-sized devices that monitor individuals from above and infiltrate even the most private spaces. These devices, designed to mimic real birds and insects, are deceptively inconspicuous, making them nearly invisible to the untrained eye.

Bird drones are typically equipped with high-resolution cameras, motion sensors, and sometimes even scent detectors, allowing them to monitor a subject without raising suspicion. Their design—modeled to resemble pigeons, crows, or other urban birds—enables them to blend seamlessly into cityscapes. By flying above crowded streets, these drones provide real-time video feeds to intelligence agencies, tracking individuals' movements and activities without any apparent signs of surveillance. As a result, they have become standard tools in urban environments where traditional monitoring methods might be detected.

Even more concerning are micro-insect drones, which imitate the appearance and behavior of flies, mosquitoes, and other small insects. Advances in nanotechnology have allowed these drones to carry miniature cameras, microphones, and even chemical sensors, enabling them to access homes, offices, and public spaces without detection. Their small size and natural appearance allow them to navigate tight spaces, such as air vents or window cracks, granting them entry into private areas. Combined with artificial intelligence for real-time facial recognition, these micro-insect drones can identify and follow specific individuals, capture conversations, observe behaviors, and transmit sensitive data back to intelligence networks. In the hands of powerful entities, these insect-sized drones effectively create an all-seeing eye, erasing the concept of privacy.

Surveillance has firmly entrenched itself on our roads with the rise of self-driving cars and high-tech vehicles like Tesla. Many modern cars, marketed as safety features, are effectively transformed into mobile surveillance units. High-definition cameras on cars record the driver, pedestrians, other vehicles, and the surrounding environment. Self-driving technology, guided by advanced artificial intelligence, processes this visual data in real-time, analyzing everything from nearby vehicles to the faces of passersby.

While these cameras are marketed as features for driver safety, they effectively transform vehicles into mobile surveillance units. High-definition cameras on cars record the driver, pedestrians, other vehicles, and the surrounding environment. Self-driving technology, guided by advanced artificial intelligence, processes this visual data in real-time, analyzing everything from nearby vehicles to the faces of passersby. This information could be invaluable to intelligence agencies, revealing individuals' routines, frequently visited locations and social connections.

Government agencies or hackers could potentially access this data, making it a powerful tool for surveillance. Self-driving cars track where people go and document when they leave, who they are with, and what they encounter. With AI-driven navigation systems continuously monitoring drivers' movements, the data collected creates a comprehensive profile of an individual's habits, networks, and lifestyle, all stored within the vehicle's onboard systems.

Robot Eyes and Surveillance in Artificial Intelligence: As robotics become more common in public and private settings, another form of surveillance emerges: robots with AI-powered cameras and tracking capabilities. Many modern robots have cameras embedded in their "eyes," which capture high-definition footage, track faces, and analyze body language. Advanced AI algorithms allow these robotic eyes to recognize individuals, record interactions, and assess emotional responses, making them invaluable tools for gathering intelligence.

Often marketed as customer service assistants or security tools, robots equipped with military-grade AI are discreet surveillance devices capable of collecting extensive data on individuals. In hospitals, airports, shopping centers, and other public spaces, robots use AI to gather data on behavior, movements, and interactions. This data may be relayed to central databases, which can be analyzed and used to build profiles of those interacting with the robots. Some robots can even recognize specific individuals, compiling their visits and interactions records.

These robots could serve as unobtrusive data collectors in the wrong hands or under deep-state directives. Robots stationed in retail spaces could monitor shopping behaviors, preferences, and even emotional responses, all feeding back to an intelligence network that analyzes data for patterns and insights. While these robots are presented as helpful assistants, they blur the line between service and surveillance, contributing to a system that records and monitors without the individual's knowledge or consent.

The Role of AI in Surveillance and Behavioral Control

Traditional surveillance typically relies on cameras and monitoring tools. However, artificial intelligence (AI) has advanced this field by transforming surveillance into a mechanism for predicting and influencing behavior. AI processes large amounts of data collected from various sources in real-time, enabling intelligence agencies to analyze patterns, identify trends, and accurately predict actions. This represents a significant shift from simple observation to proactive monitoring, anticipating threats, and controlling behavior before incidents occur.

AI and Data Analysis: At the core of modern surveillance, AI sifts through massive amounts of data and detects patterns. Whether video footage from urban cameras, GPS data from smartphones, or online activity logs, AI algorithms can process and cross-reference information, identifying correlations that would otherwise be impossible for humans to detect. This technology powers everything from predictive policing to threat assessment systems, creating a network of intelligence that can analyze not just individual actions but societal trends.

One primary application of AI in surveillance is predictive policing, which uses historical data and real-time inputs to forecast where crimes are likely to occur. For example, algorithms might analyze crime statistics, weather patterns, social media posts, and even economic indicators to predict future hotspots of criminal activity. While proponents argue that predictive policing helps prevent crime, critics warn that it can lead to biased, preemptive policing tactics. Relying on data to forecast behavior blurs the line between prevention and profiling, especially when AI-driven predictions lead to action without any actual offense being committed.

Facial Recognition and Biometrics: A cornerstone of AI-powered surveillance is facial recognition, a technology that identifies individuals based on unique facial characteristics. With high-resolution cameras and advanced AI-driven analysis, facial recognition software can capture and match images of individuals in real time, using databases that contain millions of faces. This technology has quickly spread beyond military and intelligence agencies, finding applications in commercial spaces, public transportation systems, and schools.

While facial recognition is often justified as a tool for improving safety, its pervasiveness means that anonymity in public spaces is disappearing. People moving through cities, airports, and shopping centers can now be identified, tracked, and analyzed based on facial features alone. Combined with AI, these systems don't just identify individuals; they monitor expressions, body language, and even potential emotional states, creating a profile far beyond physical appearance. Critics argue that such capabilities erode privacy and freedom to move through society without constant scrutiny.

Behavioral Profiling and Predictive Analysis: AI surveillance systems can now assess behavioral patterns beyond simple identification. Using machine learning models, these systems analyze individuals' movements, gestures, and speech patterns to detect behaviors that may signify specific intentions or emotions. For instance, AI may flag individuals exhibiting nervous body language, irregular eye movements, or unusual route patterns, marking them as potential risks in real time.

Such technology is ubiquitous in high-security environments like airports, but the potential applications go much further. Theoretically, any public space could deploy AI-driven behavioral profiling, alerting authorities to suspicious behaviors. The problem with such systems lies in their tendency to misinterpret context, particularly when profiles are built based on algorithms trained on biased data. Moreover, once an individual's behavior is flagged, they may unknowingly become a subject of further surveillance, effectively placing them under suspicion without their knowledge.

The Birth of the Nanny State

As AI surveillance systems expand, the justifications for their presence have grown increasingly tied to the notion of the "nanny state"—a concept wherein the government positions itself as a guardian, watching over the populace and ensuring safety by monitoring compliance. Framed as a benevolent measure, the nanny state represents an ideological shift toward constant observation in the name of "protecting" citizens. Yet, this mentality comes at a cost: freedom of thought, movement, and privacy are gradually eroded, replaced by systems that view every individual as a potential risk in need of guidance.

Justifications for Increased Surveillance: Authorities use public safety, terrorism prevention, and crime reduction as the main justifications for implementing and expanding surveillance programs. By framing surveillance as a tool for protection, the government gains public support for methods that might otherwise be seen as intrusive. For instance, in the wake of terrorist attacks, calls for more robust security measures often lead to increased surveillance, and the cycle continues.

This justification extends beyond crime and terrorism into everyday behavior. Health monitoring, especially after the COVID-19 pandemic, became a reason for deploying new surveillance methods, tracking people's movements and interactions to reduce disease spread. While intended to ensure public safety, the overlap between health data and personal behavior raised concerns. For instance, health data that tracks a person's movements and associations could easily be repurposed, effectively creating a network that monitors physical health and controls personal actions under the guise of safety.

The Emergence of Social Credit Systems: Social credit systems are one of the clearest examples of the nanny state's influence on surveillance. Inspired by the social credit model in China, which assigns citizens scores based on their behaviors, these systems offer a method of behavioral control that rewards compliance and penalizes undesirable actions. While not officially implemented in the West, discussions around social credit-like scoring have surfaced, particularly concerning insurance rates, employment opportunities, and creditworthiness.

A social credit system tracks everything from an individual's spending habits and social media interactions to their travel history and associations. With AI's help, each action is rated, and individuals accumulate a score that impacts their access to certain privileges. In theory, those with higher scores might receive incentives like faster loan approvals or discounted insurance rates, while lower scores could lead to penalties. This form of behavioral tracking extends surveillance into personal choices, creating an environment where every action is monitored, rated, and rewarded or punished based on criteria set by unseen authorities.

For the deep state, such systems offer a subtle way to control the populace. Rather than directly imposing laws, social credit systems use incentives to nudge individuals toward compliance. Individuals may begin to self-censor in a society where every action is scored, changing behaviors to align with what is considered "good." This shift creates a culture of obedience, where the government's role as protector blurs into that of a watchful overseer, guiding choices and dictating social norms through technology.

Implications for Privacy and Freedom

As the surveillance state expands, so does its influence over personal privacy and autonomy. The emergence of bird drones, insect-sized spy devices, vehicle cameras, and facial recognition AI means that privacy is becoming increasingly elusive, and the right to move through society anonymously is slipping away. Every interaction, movement, and decision is recorded, analyzed, and cataloged, creating an environment where the watchful eye of an unseen observer subtly but constantly shapes behavior.

The Loss of Privacy and Autonomy: Privacy has long been considered a cornerstone of freedom, allowing individuals the space to think, act, and express themselves without external interference. However, as sur-veillance technology penetrates deeper into everyday life, this fundamental freedom is increasingly con-strained. Surveillance drones hover overhead, self-dri-ving cars log every journey, and AI-driven facial recognition tracks individuals in public spaces. This reality affects what people do and how they feel—knowing they are being watched can lead individuals to self-censor, modifying their behavior out of fear that even innocuous actions could be misinterpreted.

The constant presence of surveillance tools creates a chilling effect on personal freedom. Where once peo-ple could move through society with a reasonable ex-pectation of anonymity, today, they are subject to scrutiny at every turn. For some, this pervasive sur-veillance means adjusting their habits or avoiding cer-tain activities, effectively policing themselves in re-sponse to the knowledge that their actions are not private. The result is a culture of compliance, where individuals act not out of genuine choice but because they feel compelled by an unseen, omnipresent au-thority.

Data as a Tool of Manipulation: Data collected through these methods is used to monitor and manip-ulate. With AI, surveillance systems can go beyond observation to influence public opinion and behavior actively. Through targeted ads, curated news feeds, and even social media algorithms, data has become a powerful tool for shaping perceptions, often without the individual's awareness. For instance, someone who frequently interacts with particular online content might find themselves surrounded by similar viewpoints, reinforcing a specific narrative or belief system.

This subtle form of control extends beyond online spaces. In the real world, surveillance data influences the design of urban spaces, the flow of traffic, and even the location of certain businesses. Using behavioral data, cities can create zones that encourage specific actions, nudging people toward "desirable" behaviors and away from problematic areas. While these measures are often justified as improvements for public order, they also represent a method of control that influences people's choices without their complete understanding.

Data manipulation is particularly concerning in the context of AI-driven behavioral profiling, which can identify individuals' vulnerabilities and tailor content accordingly. For instance, surveillance data could be used to exploit people's fears or insecurities, subtly pushing them toward behaviors that align with the goals of those in power. As surveillance becomes more sophisticated, the potential for AI to manipulate human behavior becomes not just a theoretical risk but a pressing concern.

The Future of Freedom in an Age of Surveillance

The rise of a surveillance network that includes bird drones, micro-insect spies, self-driving vehicle cameras, and AI-equipped robots signals a new age where the boundaries of privacy and freedom are continuously shrinking. What began as a method to enhance safety and security has evolved into a far-reaching web of observation guided by artificial intelligence and integrated into every corner of daily life. This ecosystem of surveillance tools has created a reality where privacy is no longer an expectation but an anomaly, and every action is a potential data point in an endless stream of monitored behavior.

The implications for personal freedom are profound. As surveillance technology advances, the line between security and control blurs, giving rise to a world where the government and its supporting agencies watch over citizens with unprecedented detail. The concept of a nanny state—an authority that monitors and guides "for our own good"—has moved from theory to reality, where citizens are subtly controlled and influenced in ways they may not even recognize.

As this surveillance network grows, society faces a critical question: Can freedom genuinely exist in an age of constant observation? If every action, every movement, and every decision is tracked, the essence of liberty becomes compromised. In this new reality, privacy is sacrificed in the name of safety, and the ability to move through life unmonitored becomes a luxury of the past.

Looking to the future, the expansion of surveillance technology poses a challenge to the very foundation of personal liberty. In a society where the state sees all, individuality, autonomy, and freedom are inevitably compromised. In this digital panopticon, the freedom to think, act, and be without constant scrutiny may become a distant memory.

Chapter 5

The Fabrication of Reality: Media Manipulation and Information War

In the age of information, perception is everything. The deep state, wielding its most significant tool-the power to shape narratives, control the flow of information, and manipulate what people believe, is a dominant force. With mainstream media outlets, social media platforms, and a complex web of psychological operations, the deep state has turned the information landscape into a battleground. News is no longer merely reported; it is crafted, tailored, and distributed to evoke specific emotions and responses, subtly steering public opinion and fostering a manufactured reality.

This manipulation goes far beyond simple bias. Today's media ecosystem has become a sophisticated network where news, opinions, and "facts" are selectively chosen to reinforce certain beliefs while suppressing or discrediting opposing viewpoints. By controlling the narrative, the deep state constructs a world where reality is fluid, molded by those who hold the power to manipulate information. As this carefully crafted reality subsumes more aspects of society, the public becomes increasingly disconnected from objective truth, making independent thought a rare and precious commodity. This chapter explores how this network operates, the mechanisms used to influence public perception, and the psychological tools that have transformed the media into an instrument of control.

The Centralization of Media and the Decline of Independent Journalism

In recent decades, the media landscape has undergone a dramatic transformation. While the proliferation of digital platforms and news outlets gives the impression of diversity, the reality is that a handful of massive corporations control the vast majority of mainstream news sources. This consolidation of media ownership has not only enabled a narrow set of voices to dominate public discourse but also significantly limited the diversity of viewpoints. Today, a few corporate giants hold ownership stakes in nearly every major news network, newspaper, and radio station, creating a media environment far more unified in its messaging than it appears on the surface.

Corporate Control of Mainstream Media: The consolidation of media ownership can be traced back to the late 20th century when deregulation in the United States allowed corporations to acquire more extensive media holdings. Previously, media ownership restrictions helped ensure that various voices contributed to public debate, preventing any single entity from monopolizing the flow of information. However, as these restrictions were relaxed, major corporations acquired multiple outlets across print, broadcast, and digital platforms. Today, six corporations control roughly 90% of the media landscape, a reality that enables an unprecedented level of narrative control.

This centralization makes it easier for those in power to craft consistent messages across various media platforms. When these corporations report the news, their narratives often align closely, reinforcing each other in a coordinated manner. If a particular story or interpretation of events is unfavorable to the interests of these media conglomerates or their backers, it is quickly downplayed, reframed, or ignored. Conversely, narratives that support these interests are amplified, repeated across networks, and positioned as "undisputed facts." By limiting access to diverse viewpoints, these media corporations have created an echo chamber that distorts reality and promotes agendas favorable to the powers behind them.

The Death of Independent Journalism: Consolidating media ownership has devastated independent journalism, particularly investigative reporting. As corporations increasingly prioritize profit and efficiency, many newsrooms have experienced drastic cuts to their investigative reporting budgets. Independent journalists who once uncovered corruption, held leaders accountable, and brought suppressed stories to light have been sidelined, their work replaced by "repeat journalism." This decline in investigative journalism means that stories challenging the official narrative are less likely to receive coverage. Dissenting voices that once had a place in independent media are now primarily confined to smaller, often marginalized platforms.

This decline in investigative journalism means that stories challenging the official narrative are less likely to receive coverage. Dissenting voices that once had a place in independent media are now primarily confined to smaller, often marginalized platforms. When independent journalists attempt to break controversial stories that contradict mainstream narratives, they face obstacles ranging from financial difficulties to outright censorship. For those seeking information outside the official story, this media landscape is a minefield where objective truth is increasingly difficult to discern.

Operation Mockingbird and Media Assets: The deep state's influence on media narratives goes far beyond corporate ownership. Since the Cold War, the CIA has actively sought to shape public opinion through programs like Operation Mockingbird, which involved recruiting journalists as conduits for government-approved narratives. Initially, this program was designed to counter Soviet influence, but it quickly expanded into a broader operation aimed at managing how Americans viewed global and domestic events.

Operation Mockingbird involved dozens of journalists, editors, and media executives who were paid to present information favorable to U.S. government interests. Over time, this program was officially disbanded, but its legacy lives on. Today, it is no secret that intelligence agencies continue to exert influence over media narratives. In the modern iteration of Mockingbird, the deep state has strategically positioned individuals within significant media organizations as talking heads, anchors, and analysts. These media personalities subtly steer public perception, framing stories, using selective language, and emphasizing certain narratives to mold public opinion.

These assets ensure the mainline narrative aligns with deep-state interests when news breaks. These media figures maintain control over the public's understanding of events, whether through headlines that stir specific emotional responses or expert commentary that discourages dissent. By blending fact with carefully crafted commentary, they construct narratives that serve particular agendas, often supporting interventions, policy changes, or shifts in public opinion that benefit those in power. Today, the legacy of Operation Mockingbird endures, with the media serving as both a tool for information and a mechanism for control.

Psychological Operations and the Shaping of Public Opinion

With the media landscape tightly controlled, psychological operations (or "psyops") are used to shape public opinion subtly but powerfully. These operations use classic propaganda techniques, updated with modern insights into human psychology, to influence emotions, reinforce existing biases, and polarize the public. The objective is to inform and direct thoughts, behaviors, and beliefs in ways that serve specific agendas. In elections, during crises, and even daily news cycles, these methods create a manufactured consensus that aligns with the interests of those who control the narrative.

The Use of Propaganda Techniques: Propaganda has evolved significantly since its early use in wartime, but many core tactics remain the same. Today, these techniques are bolstered by psychological insights into what triggers human emotions and reactions. Repetition, for instance, is a cornerstone of modern propaganda. By repeatedly exposing the public to a particular narrative, media outlets create a sense of familiarity and certainty around specific viewpoints. The more often people hear a message, the more likely they accept it as truth—a phenomenon known as the "illusory truth effect."

Another common tactic is framing, in which facts are selectively presented to lead audiences toward specific conclusions. News coverage may focus disproportionately on certain aspects of a story while ignoring others, subtly shaping public perception without the need for outright deception. For example, when covering social unrest, media may highlight scenes of violence or property damage, focusing less on the motivations behind the protests or the socioeconomic factors contributing to public anger. This selective presentation frames the demonstrations in a particular light, steering the public's response without ever telling an outright falsehood.

Appealing to emotion is another technique that has become central to psychological operations. Fear, outrage, and empathy are powerful motivators, and media stories often aim to evoke these emotions to guide public opinion. Images of tragedy, stories of heroism, and sensational headlines create strong emotional reactions that bypass logical analysis. By tapping into these emotional responses, those in control of the narrative can manipulate the public's perception of events and sway opinion in subtle but profound ways.

Swaying Elections and Political Popularity: The use of propaganda intensifies during election seasons, when the stakes are highest, and public opinion can swing wildly in response to media narratives. Through selective reporting, framing, and repeated exposure to particular themes, media outlets can drastically alter the perception of a political candidate. By emphasizing a candidate's perceived strengths or weaknesses, mainstream media can make or break a politician's reputation.

During elections, positive or negative coverage of candidates often mirrors the preferences of corporate or political interests. A candidate who threatens the status quo may find themselves at the center of a media firestorm, with stories focusing on perceived flaws, controversies, or blunders. Conversely, candidates who align with the deep state's interests are frequently depicted as competent, relatable, and trustworthy, with negative stories minimized or ignored. This asymmetry in media coverage creates an uneven playing field, where popular support is artificially bolstered or diminished by the media's portrayal.

Moreover, specific narratives can be amplified to endear or demonize a candidate. Scandals, whether credible or exaggerated, become tools to sway the electorate. If a narrative is repeated enough, it becomes ingrained in the public's mind as fact, regardless of the evidence. Through these techniques, media can play a decisive role in shaping election outcomes and influencing political popularity, ensuring that candidates aligned with specific agendas have a significant advantage over their rivals.

Social Media Algorithms and Echo Chambers: Beyond traditional media, social media platforms now serve as significant arenas for psychological operations, where algorithms and echo chambers reinforce specific narratives. Social media algorithms are designed to maximize engagement, prioritizing content that aligns with users' existing beliefs and preferences. This creates "echo chambers," where users are primarily exposed to information confirming their viewpoints, isolating them from alternative perspectives. Over time, these echo chambers solidify beliefs, making individuals more resistant to opposing viewpoints and more susceptible to the narratives promoted within their online circles.

In these echo chambers, social media platforms exert considerable influence over what users see and how they think. Platforms amplify ideological divides by curating content that reinforces biases, pushing users further into polarized groups. This polarization serves the interests of those who control the platforms, as a divided populace is more straightforward to manipulate and control. When people are divided and isolated in ideological silos, they are less likely to unite against common issues and more likely to direct their frustrations at each other.

Social media platforms often employ algorithms prioritizing sensational or emotionally charged content, as these posts drive higher engagement. Consequently, narratives that provoke fear, anger, or outrage are more likely to spread widely, creating a cycle of emotionally charged responses that influence public perception. The result is a manipulated reality where users are constantly bombarded with messages that align with specific agendas, reinforcing a controlled narrative while suppressing dissenting voices.

The Weaponization of "Fake News" and the Control of Information

In recent years, "fake news" has gained significant attention, transforming from a phrase describing misinformation to a powerful tool for discrediting opposition and controlling narratives. While "fake news" originally referred to false or misleading information, it has since become a weaponized term, used to label any narrative that challenges the preferred storyline of the mainstream or counters deep state interests.

Through this redefinition, those in power can undermine stories and perspectives they find inconvenient, labeling them as fabrications and, in turn, swaying public perception.

Fake News and Disinformation Campaigns: The concept of "fake news" plays a dual role in modern information warfare. First, it serves as a label to discredit dissenting voices. When a narrative, story, or piece of information threatens the interests of the deep state or corporate entities, it can be quickly dismissed by labeling it as "fake news." This tactic is particularly effective because it requires minimal justification; an unadorned accusation can doubt a story's credibility, even if it contains factual information.

Second, actual disinformation campaigns are sometimes orchestrated to muddy the waters and create confusion around particular issues. By seeding a mix of natural and false information, intelligence agencies or private interests can lead the public to distrust legitimate details and narratives. For example, in times of political tension, stories with false claims are sometimes disseminated alongside legitimate ones, making it difficult for the public to discern fact from fiction. Over time, this blending of information and disinformation creates an environment where individuals are left unsure of what to believe, making them more vulnerable to manipulation.

Fact-Checking and Censorship: Fact-checking organizations have risen in prominence as arbiters of truth, claiming to protect the public from false information. However, many of these organizations are backed by corporate interests, government agencies, or other entities with vested interests. Rather than serving as neutral bodies, these fact-checkers often exhibit bias, selectively labeling information as true or false based on how it aligns with the mainstream narrative.

For instance, information that contradicts a preferred storyline may be labeled as "false" or "misleading," even if it contains elements of truth. In contrast, stories supporting the mainstream narrative may be labeled as "true" despite oversimplifications or omissions. This selective fact-checking creates a one-sided picture of reality that benefits the status quo and stifles alternative viewpoints.

Fact-checking can also serve as a form of soft censorship. When stories are labeled as "false" or "misleading," they are often deprioritized on social media platforms, making them less visible to the public. Sometimes, fact-checking labels are even used to justify removing posts or accounts entirely. This approach allows platforms and fact-checkers to control which narratives reach the public without overtly silencing voices, effectively making censorship appear as a necessary public service.

Shadow-Banning on Social Media: Shadow-banning is another tool social media platforms use to suppress certain viewpoints subtly. Unlike outright bans, shadow-banning restricts content visibility without alerting users that their posts are limited. In practice, shadow-banning involves making specific posts or accounts less visible, causing them to receive fewer interactions and reach fewer people. For the user, they are sharing content with the world, but their reach is quietly stifled behind the scenes.

Shadow banning is particularly insidious because it targets individuals based on the ideas they express, often silencing voices that run counter to the dominant narrative. Accounts that post about controversial topics or question mainstream beliefs are more likely to experience shadow-banning, limiting the public's exposure to alternative ideas. By selectively suppressing dissent, social media platforms can shape the public discourse to reflect a unified narrative, reinforcing the messages approved by those in power.

While platforms justify shadow-banning as a way to manage "harmful" or "misleading" content, this practice grants significant power to those who determine what qualifies as "harmful." The result is an information ecosystem where diversity of thought is subtly but steadily reduced, leading to a reality where only sanctioned perspectives are widely visible. For the average user, the effects of shadow-banning are invisible but profound, as fewer and fewer ideas outside the mainstream narrative make it into their social feeds.

Surveillance, Targeted Information, and Individual Targeting

Collecting and analyzing personal data have become ubiquitous, with individuals' every move, interaction, and preference recorded and cataloged. Originally marketed as tools for enhancing convenience and personalization, these data-gathering methods now serve a dual purpose, providing deep-state and corporate interests with unprecedented access to private lives. This wealth of information, from purchasing habits to online search history, is analyzed and used to influence, manipulate, and control individuals. At its most invasive, this data becomes a weapon for targeted surveillance and intimidation, often carried out by a web of FBI Infragard agents, private targeting companies, and blackmailed citizens.

Accumulation of Private Information for Influence: Social media platforms, search engines, and other online services collect detailed profiles of every user, from interests and relationships to location data and browsing history. While this information is often presented to provide targeted advertising, it is also used to build profiles that predict and shape an individual's behavior. Through data analysis and machine learning, corporations and government entities gain insights into an individual's psychological profile, personal beliefs, and vulnerabilities.

Influencer campaigns can be highly personalized in a system where private information is readily available. For example, individuals who frequently search for health-related topics may receive targeted ads and information to push them toward specific products, behaviors, or viewpoints. In political contexts, this information allows those in power to deliver hyper-targeted propaganda, swaying individuals' opinions by catering to their specific fears, interests, and biases. By influencing people at such a personal level, this data-driven approach shifts the boundaries of persuasion, moving from broad-based messaging to one-on-one influence campaigns.

Targeting Individuals through Private Information: While targeted information campaigns are often subtle, surveillance tactics go beyond mere influence, extending into intimidation and harassment. For those perceived as threats to the status quo, such as activists, journalists, or political dissidents, accumulating private information can be a prelude to more aggressive forms of control. Once an individual's data is analyzed, it can be used to track, monitor, and intimidate them to stifle dissent.

In recent years, FBI Infragard agents, private targeting companies, and even citizens who have been coerced or blackmailed have been implicated in these surveillance operations. Infragard, a private-public partnership between the FBI and corporate entities, operates to promote security and prevent cyber threats. However, critics argue that it also provides the FBI with a network of private actors who assist in targeting individuals deemed dangerous to deep state interests. By working through corporate partners and private citizens, Infragard agents can gather data and conduct surveillance outside the legal constraints that apply to official law enforcement.

Private targeting companies, meanwhile, offer similar services for those who wish to harass or monitor individuals without the direct involvement of law enforcement. These companies leverage advanced surveillance technologies and data analysis to track individuals, sometimes blurring the line between security and intimidation. For those targeted, this often manifests as a constant feeling of being watched, with unknown figures tracking their movements, monitoring their communications, and infiltrating their social circles.

In some cases, even ordinary citizens become tools of surveillance and intimidation. Blackmailed or coerced by intelligence agencies or private targeting companies, these individuals may be enlisted to monitor or report on the activities of their neighbors, friends, or family members. This tactic creates a pervasive atmosphere of distrust, where even personal relation-ships are subject to manipulation by those in power. By enlisting citizens as informants, the deep state extends its reach into every aspect of private life, turning communities into networks of surveillance.

These surveillance tactics serve to keep potential dis-senters in check, leveraging personal information as a tool of psychological intimidation. The effect can be profound for individuals who are aware that they are being monitored. The knowledge that every move, conversation, and interaction is subject to observation creates a chilling effect, making people less likely to voice dissenting opinions or participate in actions that challenge the status quo.

Manufacturing Consent and Controlling Perceptions

One of the most potent tools for shaping public opin-ion is the ability to control the narrative surrounding significant events. By deciding what is emphasized, downplayed, or omitted entirely, those in control of the media can effectively manufacture consent, subtly guiding the public to accept specific interpretations and reject others. Through strategic framing and se-lective emphasis, the deep state influences what peo-ple think about and how they think about it. This technique of narrative control is a sophisticated form of psychological influence, molding public opinion to support specific agendas without direct coercion.

Framing Events to Shape Public Beliefs: Framing is a psychological technique that involves presenting information to encourage a particular interpretation. By carefully choosing language, focus, and context, the media can lead audiences to specific conclusions without overtly telling them what to think. For example, a report on a protest might highlight incidents of violence while ignoring the motivations or grievances of the protesters. This selective framing creates an impression of chaos and lawlessness, diverting attention from any legitimate concerns the protest might raise.

In international affairs, framing can be used to paint certain countries as aggressive, oppressive, or morally corrupt. Consistent coverage that emphasizes negative aspects while downplaying counterpoints gradually shapes public opinion to view these nations as enemies. In contrast, allies or partners are often portrayed positively, with coverage that emphasizes their strengths and ignores their flaws. This manipulation of public perception primes citizens to support foreign policies that align with deep-state interests, such as sanctions, interventions, or alliances, without questioning the deeper motives.

The media's role in framing also extends to domestic issues, where focusing on inevitable crises over others directs attention and resources toward specific agendas. Issues that align with powerful interests receive extensive coverage, creating a sense of urgency that demands a response. Meanwhile, issues that could challenge the status quo are often ignored, marginalized, or dismissed as irrelevant. By controlling what the public sees, hears, and ultimately cares about, the media ensures that the deep state's priorities remain unchallenged.

Creating Villains and Heroes: Another critical technique in narrative control is the establishment of clear-cut villains and heroes. By simplifying complex issues into moral stories with "good" and "bad" actors, the media makes it easier for the public to form strong emotional attachments to specific figures and positions. This tactic is especially effective in a politically polarized society, where the need for moral clarity often overrides critical thinking.

Villains are typically figures or groups that oppose the deep state's agenda or threaten established power structures. These individuals or organizations are portrayed as dangerous, corrupt, or morally bankrupt through constant negative coverage, effectively alienating them from the general public. Over time, this consistent portrayal leads the public to view these figures as threats to social order, justifying harsh responses, whether through public shaming, legal action, or even violence. For example, activists, whistleblowers, or dissenting political figures often become targets, with media coverage emphasizing any flaws or controversies that can be used to undermine their credibility.

In contrast, heroes are carefully crafted figures who embody the values the deep state wishes to promote. These individuals are often positioned as protectors, reformers, or voices of reason, receiving positive media coverage that highlights their accomplishments and minimizes their faults. The media creates role models by establishing specific figures as heroes, shaping public expectations, and inspiring support for particular policies. Whether in politics, entertainment, or activism, these heroes serve as rallying points for public sentiment, guiding people toward certain beliefs and away from others.

This "villain and hero" dichotomy also polarizes society, reinforcing divides that keep the public focused on battling one another rather than questioning those in power. By creating clear sides and casting figures in black-and-white terms, the media ensures that audiences are more likely to adopt extreme positions, further fracturing society and preventing unity on critical issues. In a world dominated by such narratives, critical thinking is replaced by emotional reactions, making the public more susceptible to manipulation and less capable of challenging the underlying forces at play.

The Battle for Reality in the Age of Information

In an era where perception is paramount, the power to shape reality lies in controlling the narrative. Through media centralization, psychological operations, selective framing, and the careful crafting of villains and heroes, the deep state has established a powerful apparatus for manipulating public opinion. In this environment, truth becomes a matter of perspective, molded by those controlling information flow. As society becomes increasingly fragmented and divided, the public's understanding of reality becomes fractured, making it difficult for individuals to see the broader patterns of control at play.

The consequences of this manufactured reality are profound. When narratives are controlled, and dissenting voices are marginalized, independent thought becomes an act of resistance. In a world where the truth is what those in power say it is, seeking genuine understanding falls to those willing to look beyond the headlines, question the official story, and seek alternative perspectives. In this age of information warfare, the battle for reality is ongoing, and the stakes are nothing less than the future of personal freedom and the public's ability to think critically about the world around them.

For those willing to resist the pull of the mainstream narrative, the first step is awareness: recognizing the methods of manipulation at play, questioning the motives behind the stories, and seeking out voices that challenge the status quo. In a world where media manipulation is omnipresent, the ability to discern truth from fiction is a revolutionary act that empowers individuals to reclaim their autonomy and resist the forces that seek to control their minds.

Chapter 6

Beyond Borders: Global Alliances and the Web of Control

In the era of globalization, it's crucial to recognize that decisions made by foreign powers and international organizations are not detached from our daily lives. A closer examination reveals a complex and powerful web of alliances, covert collaborations, and transnational power structures that operate beyond national boundaries. These global networks—intelligence-sharing agreements, corporate partnerships, and foreign-controlled assets—wield significant influence over nations, shaping their policies and directly impacting the lives of their citizens. While these influences can be concerning, it's important to note that these alliances and organizations also play a crucial role in promoting global security, cooperation, and humanitarianism.

This covert network operates with little oversight from individual countries, often shrouded in secrecy and lacking accountability. Central to this system are alliances like the Five Eyes intelligence-sharing group and organizations such as the United Nations and the World Health Organization. Although these entities were established to promote global security, cooperation, and humanitarianism, they have accrued powers far exceeding their original mandates. With their extensive reach, they enforce policies that affect everything from citizens' rights to national security, such as the right to privacy in the digital age and the right to make independent health decisions. This creates a globalized system where sovereignty is undermined by centralized control.

Intelligence-Sharing Alliances and the Five Eyes Network

The Five Eyes alliance, a pivotal player in international surveillance and information sharing, is a coalition of the United States, the United Kingdom, Canada, Australia, and New Zealand. Established during the Cold War to monitor and counter Soviet influence, the Five Eyes alliance has evolved into one of the world's most extensive and sophisticated surveillance networks. Each member nation collects intelligence on its citizens and allies, effectively bypassing individual national privacy laws to create a global surveillance system with virtually no blind spots, a system that reverberates across the globe.

The Origins and Evolution of Five Eyes: In its early days, Five Eyes focused primarily on monitoring foreign threats, using resources from each nation to develop a comprehensive view of the Soviet Union's activities. But as technology advanced, so did the alliance's methods, and its mission expanded to include domestic surveillance under the pretext of countering terrorism, organized crime, and cyber threats. This evolution mirrors the rapid advancement of surveillance technology, turning Five Eyes into a global intelligence superpower.

The Role of Five Eyes Today: The alliance's strength lies in its collaborative model, where each member country contributes data collected through its domestic programs. For example, while U.S. intelligence agencies like the NSA may face restrictions on surveilling American citizens, the Five Eyes alliance allows them to access similar data through their counterparts in the U.K. or Australia. This arrangement enables member nations to navigate their privacy laws, creating a global surveillance network that extends into nearly every aspect of individuals' lives. Whether it involves monitoring phone calls, browsing histories, or physical movements, the Five Eyes network closely monitors the global population, quietly gathering data that feeds into its extensive intelligence apparatus.

Today, Five Eyes continues to adapt its methods, incorporating new technology like AI-driven facial recognition, predictive analytics, and deep-learning algorithms capable of anticipating behaviors. What was once a defense against foreign powers has become an all-encompassing surveillance system, extending its influence into every corner of modern life. For those within its reach, privacy has become an illusion, a casualty of a borderless intelligence network designed to monitor and, if necessary, control its subjects.

The United Nations, the World Health Organization, and the New World Order Agenda

In times of crisis—such as a global pandemic, natural disaster, or humanitarian emergency—international organizations like the United Nations (U.N.) and the World Health Organization (WHO) often play crucial roles in providing coordination and aid. While these organizations are praised for their humanitarian efforts, a closer look reveals a different aspect of their influence. Through broad mandates and extensive pU.N.cols, the U.N. and WHO have established mechanisms that can, under certain conditions, override national laws and infringe upon citizens' rights. Their stated goals of promoting peace, health, and security have, in practice, created a framework that allows for control over populations, all under the pretense of protection.

U.N. and WHO as Vehicles of Global Control: The U.N. was initially created to prevent another world war, serving as a forum where countries could come together to discuss and resolve their differences. However, the U.N.'s reach has expanded far beyond its original purpose. Over time, the organization has gained powers that allow it to influence—and, in some cases, dictate—domestic policies. In recent years, the WHO has joined in this trend, using health crises to implement international guidelines that often supersede the policies of sovereign nations. These protocols are frequently adopted without public scrutiny, creating situations where international regulations rather than national laws bind citizens.

Pandemics, Crises, and the Push for Compliance: During the COVID-19 pandemic, the WHO's role in directing the global response became more pronounced. Through advisories, guidelines, and recommendations, the WHO set protocols that influenced government actions worldwide, ranging from mask mandates to lockdown policies. In the name of public health, these guidelines created a framework for controlling behavior, monitoring individuals, and, in some cases, enforcing severe restrictions on personal free-dom, a framework that was felt by individuals and governments alike.

Through actions, the WHO and U.N. are often seen as mechanisms for promoting a New World Order agen-da, pushing for centralized control across multiple na-tions. By setting international protocols, these organi-zations establish precedents that can be used to justify control measures in the future. Each crisis sets the stage for the next, subtly advancing a vision of a glob-al governance system where individual rights take a backseat to centralized authority. This potential shift in power dynamics could have significant implications for individual rights and national sovereignty, raising important questions about the balance between global cooperation and local autonomy.

The United Nations Influence Over U.S. National Parks

The influence of the United Nations within U.S. bor-ders extends beyond policies and protocols—it even reaches into the country's natural landscapes. During his presidency, Bill Clinton made several decisions that effectively handed over partial control of U.S. Na-tional Parks to the UN. Many of these parks today bear U.N. plaques at their entrances, signaling an in-ternational stake in America's most treasured natural resources. While framed as a means of preserving these lands, the involvement of the UN has more profound implications, serving as a reminder that national sovereignty can be subtly eroded in the name of global cooperation.

Bill Clinton's National Parks Decision: Clinton's decision to involve the UN in managing U.S. National Parks came with little public explanation, though it was couched regarding environmental protection. By placing these parks under UNESCO's World Heritage and Biosphere Reserve programs, Clinton essentially gave the UN a foothold within U.S. borders. The plaques placed at park entrances signify more than just a partnership—they mark a shift in control that ties these lands to an international agenda.

The Larger Agenda Behind U.N. Involvement: The presence of the U.N. in America's national parks has fueled speculation about a larger agenda. Some view this international oversight as part of a long-term strategy to erode U.S. sovereignty, preparing the way for a future where global governance supersedes national authority. With the UN's influence extending into U.S. territories, it becomes easier to establish precedents that justify increased international involvement. What may appear as an innocuous environmental initiative could serve as a stepping stone toward a more centralized global control structure that encroaches on national autonomy under the guise of preservation and sustainability.

Covert Military and Intelligence Programs

Hidden beneath the veneer of government transparency lies a complex network of covert programs funded through "black budgets" that evade public oversight. These budgets finance secret projects ranging from advanced weapons systems to untraceable military actions. By using these funds, government agencies can pursue operations that would otherwise be impossible to justify, effectively creating a parallel infrastructure that operates beyond the reach of democratic processes.

Black Budget Operations: The funds allocated to black budget programs are astronomical, often obscured within larger government spending bills to avoid scrutiny. These budgets allow for developing cutting-edge technologies, such as autonomous drones, surveillance satellites, and experimental weaponry. While some of these programs are intended for national defense, others push the boundaries of ethics and legality. The secrecy surrounding black budget operations means that the public has little knowledge of the true scope of these projects or their implications for global stability.

The Global Implications of Clandestine Military Actions: Black budget programs have created untraceable military units that can be deployed anywhere in the world without official acknowledgment.

These operatives conduct missions that, if made public, would likely spark international outrage. From assassinations to covert interventions, these actions remain off the record, allowing governments to deny responsibility. For citizens, this means living in a world where their nation's military might be engaged in actions that could have profound consequences, all without their knowledge or consent.

China's Influence within U.S. Borders and the Role of Foreign Trade Zones

China's influence within the United States goes far beyond its role as a trade partner. In recent years, Chinese entities have acquired significant stakes in major U.S. shipping ports, providing them with strategic control over critical infrastructure. These ports are gateways to America's supply chain, handling goods and resources essential to the country's economy. However, this control raises serious national security concerns, as it gives a foreign power unprecedented access to monitor, manipulate, and potentially disrupt the flow of goods into the U.S.

China's Control over Major U.S. Shipping Ports: Chinese companies have invested heavily in U.S. ports, particularly along the West Coast. This control gives them insight into American trade flows, providing valuable intelligence on everything from the timing of shipments to the types of goods being imported and exported. The implications are significant, as this control could be used to influence economic policy, gather intelligence, or even create supply chain vulnerabilities that could be exploited in times of tension or conflict.

Activities within Foreign Trade Zones (FTZs): U.S. Foreign Trade Zones in the U.S. operate under a unique set of regulations that allow certain exemptions from customs laws. Many U.S. zones near U.S. military installations create potential security risks. With vast land areas and autonomy, these FTZs are ripe for exploitation. Reports suggest that certain FTZs under Chinese control could be used for purposes beyond standard trade activities, though the specifics remain unknown. This setup raises troubling questions about foreign influence on U.S. soil, mainly when these zones operate with minimal oversight.

Secret Partnerships with Multinational Corporations

Governments and intelligence agencies have long relied on partnerships with private corporations to extend their reach, but these partnerships have become even more entrenched in recent years. Through collaborations with tech giants and private security firms, the deep state can conduct surveillance and intelligence operations that would otherwise be restricted. These corporations provide resources and a layer of deniability, allowing governments to outsource ethically questionable tasks while maintaining plausible deniability.

Tech Giants as Surveillance Extensions: Companies like Google, Amazon, and Microsoft have unparalleled access to data on individuals worldwide. These tech giants have become essential players in global surveillance through government contracts and informal partnerships. From collecting location data to monitoring internet activity, these companies enable intelligence agencies to gather information on an unprecedented scale. For individuals, this means that their data is collected and shared with entities that can use it for surveillance or even manipulation.

The Influence of Private Military and Security Companies: Private security firms like Academi (formerly Blackwater) serve as unofficial arms of government intelligence. With their personnel trained in combat, surveillance, and tactical operations, these companies can execute missions that are too controversial for direct government involvement. By using private contractors, intelligence agencies can maintain deniability, ensuring that operations remain off the books. This setup creates a shadow military that operates without the accountability or oversight typically associated with government forces.

The Globalization of Surveillance and Control Mechanisms

As international intelligence alliances, multinational corporations, and covert operations extend their influence, the infrastructure of a global surveillance state emerges. Unified databases and predictive algorithms create a network where information flows seamlessly across borders, enabling a level of surveillance that no single government could achieve alone. In this landscape, privacy, and autonomy are sacrificed for security and control as predictive policing and information-sharing initiatives expand their reach.

Unified Databases and Global Information-Sharing: By compiling personal information, financial records, and travel histories into centralized databases, intelligence agencies create a global surveillance apparatus. These databases allow governments to monitor individuals regardless of nationality, maintaining comprehensive records that can be accessed by law enforcement across borders. This network erodes privacy, subjecting individuals to scrutiny no matter where they are.

Predictive Policing and International Law Enforcement Collaboration: Predictive policing initiatives use algorithms to monitor individuals and identify potential threats before they materialize. While these programs claim to prevent crime, they also create an environment of constant surveillance, where individuals are judged not only by their actions but by the potential for deviance. International collaborations expand this reach, allowing agencies to track individuals globally, furthering the scope of the surveillance state.

The Rise of a Global Surveillance State

The emergence of a global surveillance state reveals a shift in power from governments to a network of international alliances, corporations, and covert entities. As these structures solidify, personal freedom and privacy become casualties of a new era of centralized control. The global surveillance web is no longer confined to science fiction; it is an established reality designed to monitor and influence individuals without their knowledge.

In a world where borders no longer protect privacy, the question of autonomy becomes more pressing. For those who wish to resist the grip of this globalized power, the task is daunting, requiring constant vigilance and a willingness to question the systems that shape their lives. As the global surveillance state grows, so does the need for individuals to reclaim their autonomy, challenging the forces that seek to control their minds, actions, and futures.

Part 2: Cosmic Forces and Ancient Prophecies

Chapter 7

Nemesis Revealed: The Mystery of Planet X

Humanity has gazed at the heavens for millennia, seeking answers to life's greatest mysteries. The celestial realm has inspired myths, religions, and scientific inquiry, offering insights into our past and glimpses of a potential future. Yet hidden among the stars is one of our solar system's most enigmatic and debated entities: Planet X, known to the ancient Sumerians as Nibiru. This massive celestial body, shrouded in secrecy and controversy, is believed to be the Nemesis to our Sun—a burnt-out brown dwarf star that may one day return to disrupt the delicate balance of the cosmos.

Described in ancient Sumerian cylinder seals that date back 8,000 years, Nibiru is not just a planet but a harbinger of cataclysmic change. Some researchers, including my good friend Dr. Jaysen Rand, theorize that Nibiru is a binary companion to our Sun. If true, this would place our solar system, among many others, in the universe believed to have two stars. As Nibiru continues its fateful journey, its gravitational influence could disrupt planetary alignments, unleash devastating natural disasters, and fulfill ancient prophecies foretelling the end of an era.

The Modern Discovery of Planet X

The search for a tenth planet (now considered by modern astronomers as the ninth planet)—or, in this case, a rogue celestial body—dates back to the late 19th century, when astronomers observed unexplained anomalies in the orbits of Neptune and Uranus. These irregularities suggested the presence of a massive, undiscovered object lurking at the fringes of our solar system. By the early 20th century, this hypothetical planet was dubbed "Planet X," derived from the Roman numeral for ten, reflecting its status as the solar system's tenth planet.

In 1930, astronomer Clyde Tombaugh discovered Pluto while searching for Planet X. For much of the 20th century, Pluto retained its status as the ninth planet, leaving Planet X as the theoretical tenth planet. However, in 2006, the International Astronomical Union (IAU) controversially reclassified Pluto as a dwarf planet, removing it from the list of major planets. This adjustment repositioned Planet X as the ninth planet—a change many argue was deliberately framed to confuse new and unwitting researchers who might otherwise uncover deeper truths about the Nemesis star system.

Coincidentally, Clyde Tombaugh was an acquaintance of my father's father. My father once shared a fascinating story about a dinner he had as a young boy with his father and the famed astronomer. At the dinner table, Tombaugh and my grandfather engaged in a lively conversation about the nature of gravity. As my father recalls, Tombaugh entertained the provocative idea, suggested by my grandfather, that "gravity is merely created by atmospheric pressure." Whether it was a serious scientific theory or a philosophical musing, the conversation left a lasting impression on my father, who relayed it to me with great intrigue years later. This anecdote adds a deeply personal connection to the broader story of Tombaugh's contributions to astronomy and the mystery of Planet X.

Despite his groundbreaking discovery, Pluto's small size and low mass quickly ruled it out as the source of the gravitational anomalies that had initially sparked the search for Planet X. The hunt continued, leading to new theories and observations that pushed the boundaries of conventional astronomy.

Unlike the other planets, which orbit the Sun directly, Planet X—or Nibiru—belongs to a separate star system. It revolves around its failed sun named Nemesis, a burnt-out brown dwarf star believed to be the Sun's binary companion. Believe it or not, most if not all solar systems are thought to have two suns. The Nemesis star system operates independently of the solar system's traditional planetary orbits, moving in a cosmic yin-and-yang dance. Its elliptical orbit, stretching thousands of years, has the potential to cause massive disruptions due to its gravitational pull, a theory supported by both ancient accounts and modern observations.

Planet X in Ancient Texts and Prophecies

Long before the modern scientific search for Planet X, ancient civilizations spoke of celestial bodies that played pivotal roles in shaping Earth's history. Among these, the Sumerians—arguably one of the earliest advanced civilizations—offered some of the most intriguing accounts. Their records describe a massive, wandering planet called Nibiru, which traverses the heavens in an elongated orbit and brings both creation and destruction.

According to ancient Sumerian texts, including the Enuma Elish and various cylinder seals, Nibiru is not just a planet but a cosmic force of immense significance. It is tied to the Anunnaki, a race of advanced beings said to have visited Earth in antiquity. The Sumerians depicted Nibiru as a planet with a highly elliptical orbit, taking thousands of years to complete a single revolution around the Sun. When Nibiru nears Earth, its gravitational pull is said to cause catastrophic events, such as floods, earthquakes, and volcanic eruptions—echoes found in global myths and legends.

The concept of a disruptive celestial body is not unique to the Sumerians. In the Bible, references to the "stars falling from heaven" and "the powers of the heavens being shaken" (Matthew 24:29) bear striking similarities to descriptions of Nibiru's effects. Similarly, the Mayan Long Count Calendar, which predicted the end of an age in 2012, and Hindu cosmology's cycles of destruction and renewal align with the idea of periodic cosmic upheaval.

These ancient accounts suggest that Nibiru's periodic return is part of a more excellent cosmic cycle that heralds destruction and renewal. The Anunnaki, believed by some to be extraterrestrial visitors, are said to return alongside Nibiru, observing humanity's fate and intervening at critical junctures in our history. Whether viewed as gods, advanced beings, or symbols of cosmic forces, their connection to Nibiru underscores its profound significance in human mythology.

Government Knowledge and Censorship

Despite growing evidence regarding Planet X and its potential implications, the topic remains secrecy. Government agencies and institutions, including NASA, have faced accusations of suppressing information about Nibiru and Nemesis, leading to suspicions of a cover-up.

In 1983, the Infrared Astronomical Satellite (IRAS) made headlines when it detected what some interpreted as a massive object in the solar system's outer reaches. While NASA initially acknowledged these findings, subsequent statements downplayed the discovery, labeling it a misinterpretation. Critics argue that this shift in narrative was intentional and aimed at preventing public panic. If Nibiru's approach poses a significant threat, governments might prefer withholding information and secretly allowing themselves time to prepare.

In this context, the U.S. government's Continuity of Government (COG) programs, administered by FEMA, take on new significance. Drills and stockpiling efforts, presented as preparations for natural disasters or national security threats, could also serve as readiness measures for potential events related to Nemesis. Underground bunkers, emergency response protocols, and supply chain controls suggest a level of preparedness beyond routine disaster management.

Signs in the Sky: Modern Evidence of Planet X

Recent observations provide indirect evidence for the existence of Nibiru. From unexplained anomalies in the Kuiper Belt to Earth's magnetic field shifts, these signs suggest that a massive object may influence our solar system.

Astronomers have observed unusual patterns in the orbits of trans-Neptunian objects (TNOs), which appear to cluster in ways that indicate the presence of a large, unseen body. These anomalies correspond with predictions regarding the location and mass of Planet X. Additionally, increases in meteor activity and unexpected changes in comet trajectories suggest that a gravitational force is at play.

Closer to home, Earth's magnetic field has been weakening and shifting at an accelerating pace, a phenomenon some attribute to Nibiru's gravitational effects. This weakening could leave the planet vulnerable to solar storms and other cosmic disruptions. At the same time, the increase in global seismic and volcanic activity raises questions about whether external forces are destabilizing the Earth's crust.

The Return of the Gods

As science and mythology intertwine, the mystery of Planet X presents both a warning and a revelation. If Nibiru and Nemesis are real, their return could signify a pivotal moment in Earth's history—a time of upheaval, transformation, and possibly even intervention by forces beyond our understanding. Whether these forces are cosmic, divine, or extraterrestrial, their implications challenge humanity to prepare for a future shaped by the heavens.

In the ancient Sumerian worldview, the return of Nibiru represented not just a catastrophe but also a moment of reckoning, where the fate of civilizations hung in the balance. Today, as we piece together the evidence left by ancient texts alongside modern science, the question remains: Will humanity rise to meet the challenges of a changing cosmos, or will we become the latest victims of its inexorable cycles?

New York Times Publishes 1983 Planet X Admission

In a now-famous piece published on January 30, 1983, in Section 4, Page 20 of The New York Times, the existence of Planet X—an elusive celestial body lurking beyond Neptune—was thrust into public consciousness. The article highlighted findings from NASA's Infrared Astronomical Satellite (IRAS) program, which detected a massive and mysterious object in the far reaches of our solar system. The object, described as a potential "giant gaseous planet" or even a "proton-star," immediately stirred debates within the scientific community and among the public.

The article revealed that the object was so enigmatic and distant that it did not fit within the parameters of any known celestial body at the time. The IRAS data suggested that this body could potentially be a tenth planet, giving rise to the term "Planet X," which has since become synonymous with Nibiru and the Nemesis star system. Scientists speculated that its massive size and gravitational pull could explain irregularities observed in the orbits of Uranus and Neptune, anomalies that had baffled astronomers for decades.

This publication is particularly noteworthy because it was one of the rare instances when a mainstream outlet like The New York Times openly discussed the possibility of such a planetary intruder. Following this article, interest in Planet X exploded among amateur astronomers and conspiracy theorists. However, subsequent coverage of the topic dwindled, leading many to speculate that knowledge of Planet X's existence had been deliberately suppressed to avoid mass panic.

The 1983 article remains a cornerstone for researchers and theorists who believe that Planet X is not only real but is on a trajectory that could bring it perilously close to Earth. They argue that the IRAS findings were an early warning, later buried under layers of scientific dismissal and media silence. In hindsight, this report from The New York Times may represent a rare moment of transparency, shedding light on a mystery that continues to captivate and terrify today.

Chapter 8

NASA's IRAS Mission and the Trans-Neptune Discovery

In 1983, NASA launched the Infrared Astronomical Satellite (IRAS), a revolutionary mission that fundamentally altered our understanding of the cosmos. Unlike traditional telescopes focused on visible light, IRAS operates in the infrared spectrum, enabling it to detect heat emissions from celestial objects. This critical capability allowed astronomers to uncover phenomena obscured by dust clouds and identify objects too dim to reflect sunlight. While IRAS delivered essential data on distant galaxies and newly forming stars, one discovery emerged as particularly significant: a massive object beyond Neptune, identified as a likely brown dwarf and potentially a binary companion to our Sun.

This object, later associated with the controversial concept of Nibiru, generated widespread debate and secrecy. Dubbed Nemesis, this faint, heat-emitting celestial body carries profound implications for our solar system. It follows a highly elliptical orbit, and its gravitational influence could disrupt the solar system's stability, triggering catastrophic events on Earth. As the implications of this discovery became evident, the U.S. government took extraordinary measures to study and obscure its significance, leaving the public largely unaware of this imminent and reoccurring cosmic threat.

The IRAS Mission and the Revelation of Nemesis

NASA's IRAS mission was groundbreaking. It mapped 96% of the sky in the infrared spectrum, uncovering cosmic features that conventional telescopes could not detect. Among its findings, one particular discovery captured the scientific community's attention. IRAS identified a massive, heat-emitting object located far beyond Pluto. This object was challenging to categorize, as it did not fit the definitions of a planet or a conventional star.

What Is a Brown Dwarf Star?

A brown dwarf occupies the transitional space between planets and stars. While it is too massive to be classified as a planet, it lacks the mass needed to sustain hydrogen fusion like true stars. Brown dwarfs emit faint heat that can only be detected in the infrared spectrum. One such object, dubbed Nemesis, exemplifies these characteristics; it is often referred to as a "failed star," as its dim presence remained hidden from observation until the Infrared Astronomical Satellite (IRAS) detected it. Mainstream science once highlighted this fact in *Popular Science* before it was subsequently removed from future publications by the authorities.

Surrounding Nemesis were smaller celestial bodies, including Nibiru, a massive planet accompanied by its moons. The data suggested that this star system existed independently of the Sun's planetary arrangement, adding complexity to the overall dynamics of the solar system.

Mapping the Orbit: Nemesis and Nibiru's Trajectory

After the IRAS data confirmed the existence of Nemesis, the U.S. government quietly began efforts to map its trajectory. Through black-budget operations, leading astrophysicists and geologists calculated the orbits of Nemesis, Nibiru, and their accompanying celestial bodies.

Unlike the nearly circular orbits of planets in our solar system, Nemesis and Nibiru follow highly elliptical paths. Nibiru's orbit stretches far beyond Pluto before bringing it perilously close to the Sun. Nemesis's trajectory, though broader, occasionally intersects with the solar system, influencing the orbits of planets, asteroids, and comets.

The inclination of these orbits relative to the solar system's ecliptic plane adds another layer of unpredictability. Their periodic crossings disrupt the Oort Cloud—a vast region of icy bodies—sending a barrage of comets and debris toward the inner planets.

One of the most concerning discoveries was the Nemesis System and Nibiru's potential for dual perihelion with Earth—two close approaches in a single orbital cycle. These events could trigger gravitational disturbances, causing shifts in Earth's axis, volcanic eruptions, and massive earthquakes. The combined influence of Nemesis and Nibiru poses a dual threat that could upend the planet's delicate equilibrium. The CIA declassified document titled *The Adam and Eve Story* outlines this fact.

The concept of abrupt Earth shifts, often tied to catastrophic events like pole shifts or planetary perturbations, has fascinated scientists, researchers, and conspiracy theorists for decades. Such shifts refer to the sudden displacement of Earth's crust over its molten core, leading to dramatic changes in geography, climate, and the magnetic field. Though debated within scientific circles, this phenomenon carries potential implications that could reshape our understanding of Earth's past and future.

Abrupt Earth shifts are often linked to external celestial forces, such as the gravitational pull of a massive planetary body like Planet X (Nibiru) or significant alignments within the solar system. Advocates of this theory suggest that such a shift could result in extreme geological and atmospheric disruptions, including earthquakes, volcanic eruptions, and tsunamis. Historical records, such as ancient texts and geological evidence, point to periods of sudden upheaval that may align with these theoretical shifts, lending credence to the idea that the Earth's crust has shifted abruptly in the past.

Core drilling projects around the world offer intriguing insights into this theory. By analyzing layers of sediment, ice cores, and volcanic deposits, scientists have uncovered evidence of abrupt climate changes and catastrophic events that suggest rapid shifts in Earth's environmental conditions. Core samples from the Arctic and Antarctic, for example, reveal sudden transitions between ice ages and warmer periods, changes that may correlate with significant shifts in Earth's axial tilt or magnetic field.

Core drilling has also revealed anomalies that spark further questions about Earth's interior. For instance, variations in isotopic composition and sudden spikes in volcanic activity captured in deep geological strata suggest moments of intense internal activity. These findings align with theories that abrupt Earth shifts could be triggered by changes in the flow of the molten iron core, which not only influences the planet's magnetic field but also exerts pressure on the overlying crust.

If such shifts were to occur in the modern age, they would have devastating consequences. Coastal cities could be submerged, continents could fracture, and climate patterns would be completely upended, potentially plunging humanity into a survival crisis. For this reason, abrupt Earth shifts remain a focal point of scientific inquiry and speculative narratives, with core drilling providing critical data to understand our planet's dynamic systems better.

While mainstream science often treats abrupt Earth shifts as low-probability, the growing body of geological and historical evidence suggests the need for continued investigation. The more we understand Earth's core dynamics and the factors that could influence sudden crustal movement, the better-equipped humanity will be to mitigate the potential impacts of such a cataclysmic event. Whether through the lens of ancient warnings or cutting-edge science, the concept of abrupt Earth shifts remains a sobering reminder of the planet's volatile nature.

Government Secrecy and Black-Budget Research

The discovery of Nemesis had staggering implications, prompting an immediate and secretive response. While NASA publicly dismissed the Infrared Astronomical Satellite (IRAS) findings as mere observational errors or misinterpretations, the government privately initiated a classified effort to study Nemesis and its potential impact on Earth.

Using black budgets, the government financed advanced simulations, contingency planning, and the construction of underground facilities. These initiatives fell under the Continuity of Government (COG) protocols, designed to ensure the survival of crucial personnel during catastrophic events.

Media outlets were discouraged from reporting on Nemesis, while academic journals quietly shelved related studies. The narrative was tightly controlled to prevent public panic and allow the government to prepare without interference.

Signs of Nemesis's Influence

While Nemesis and its star system remain hidden from direct observation, their effects on Earth are becoming increasingly apparent. A surge in extreme weather events and natural disasters suggests that Nemesis's gravitational pull is already destabilizing the planet.

In recent years, cities around the world have experienced biblical-level flooding, displacing millions of people and destroying infrastructure. These events have been alarmingly frequent, ranging from record-breaking rainfall in Europe to catastrophic Asian monsoons. However, mainstream media often remains silent on these disasters, attributing them solely to climate change without considering possible cosmic influences.

Hurricane Helene exemplifies the intensifying power of Earth's storms. Experts hailed it as the first-ever Category 6 hurricane, with winds exceeding 200 mph and storm surges engulfing entire coastlines. Helene's sheer force defied conventional explanations, prompting speculation about the external factors driving such anomalies.

Earth's magnetic field is weakening and shifting at an unprecedented rate, which makes the planet more vulnerable to solar storms. At the same time, global volcanic activity and earthquakes have increased, indicating that the planet's crust is under immense stress. These changes align with the gravitational disruptions anticipated as Nemesis approaches Earth's proximity.

My Role in Warning the Public

Since 2009, I have been warning people about the preparations for catastrophic events. As a guest on the Alex Jones Show, I revealed important information about the U.S. government's activating pandemic and mass fatality preparedness plans. These plans included the construction of mass graves in every major city across the country. Cemeteries were surveyed, and burial vaults were installed below ground, ready for use in the event of mass casualties. While these measures are grim, they are part of a more considerable Continuity of Government strategy to maintain control during disasters.

When the COVID-19 pandemic emerged, I observed these plans being implemented. The pandemic acted as a beta test, allowing governments to refine logistics, supply chains, and emergency protocols under the pretense of public health. However, I knew this was just the beginning—a precursor to the more significant events associated with Nemesis's approach.

While investigating the lockdowns, I produced a feature documentary, *Shackled to Silence,* which uncovers how COVID-19 was a worldwide militarized blanket operation. (I highly recommend picking up your DVD copy of the film by scanning the QR code located on the back of this book.) This operation aimed to prepare society for the challenges of cosmic events, including asteroid strikes and volcanic eruptions. The pandemic response was carefully orchestrated to place dust masks, ventilators, and emergency supplies on every street corner while reinforcing hospital and supply chain infrastructure. *Shackled to Silence* reveals these hidden agendas, making it a must-watch for anyone seeking the truth.

Preparing for Nemesis's Return

As the timeline of Nemesis's return becomes clearer, preparations continue behind the scenes. Underground facilities, supply stockpiles, and contingency protocols are quietly being activated. Yet the broader public remains unaware, left to interpret the signs through fragmented information.

With its massive size and gravitational pull, Nibiru amplifies Nemesis's effects. Its moons and debris field add an unpredictable element, increasing the potential for catastrophic impacts. Historical accounts of wandering stars causing havoc align with predictions of Nibiru's behavior, suggesting that its periodic return has shaped Earth's history.

The discovery of Nemesis and its celestial companions reveals a universe governed by cycles of creation and destruction. As the binary companion to our Sun, Nemesis embodies this duality, periodically reshaping the solar system through its gravitational influence. Its approach challenges humanity to confront forces beyond our control, forcing us to prepare for an uncertain future.

The recent surge in extreme weather, flooding, and geological instability may be the harbinger of Nemesis's return. Governments have taken steps to prepare, yet the public remains largely in the dark. As these cosmic forces draw closer, the question remains: Will humanity rise to meet this challenge, or will we succumb to the cycles of destruction that have defined our planet's history?

Chapter 9

Sumerian Prophecies: The Return of the Anunnaki

In the cradle of civilization, the ancient Sumerians definitively chronicled remarkable tales of beings known as the Anunnaki—powerful deities who descended from the heavens to shape humanity's destiny decisively. These narratives, meticulously preserved in cuneiform tablets and cylinder seals, portray the Anunnaki as creators, rulers, and judges of humanity's fate. The most compelling aspect of their mythology is the prophecy of their return, closely tied to the orbital patterns of their home planet, Nibiru, also recognized as Planet X.

The Sumerians assert that Nibiru follows an elongated orbit around the Sun, completing one cycle every

"Shar"—approximately 3,600 Earth years. When Nibiru reaches its closest approach to the Sun, it enters a range that makes travel to Earth possible. During this brief window of opportunity—which lasts about seven years—the Anunnaki are expected to journey between the two worlds. The texts indicate that these alignments herald times of profound transformation, characterized by upheaval and renewal, as the Anunnaki actively oversaw the fate of humanity.

As modern science delves into the mysteries of the celestial phenomena described by the Sumerians, the prophecy of the Anunnaki's return becomes increasingly urgent. These ancient accounts are more than mere myths; they are likely records of actual events intricately linked to the movements of Nibiru and its celestial entourage. If the Anunnaki return, they will arrive not as observers but as influential figures—whether as saviors, destroyers, or forceful influences on humanity's progress remains to be determined.

The Anunnaki in Sumerian Mythology

The Anunnaki are a crucial part of Sumerian mythology. They are depicted as powerful beings who arrived on Earth from the heavens, bringing advanced knowledge and technology. Their name, often translated as "those who came from the stars," highlights their extraterrestrial origins. According to Sumerian texts, the

Anunnaki played a significant role in the creation of humanity and in shaping early civilizations' physical and cultural landscape.

In the Sumerian creation story, specifically the Enuma Elish, it is claimed that the Anunnaki manipulated the genetic material of existing hominids to create humans as laborers for their projects on Earth. Humanity was tasked with working in mines and fields to extract valuable resources, particularly gold, which the Anunnaki allegedly needed for the survival of their home planet. This narrative has drawn parallels to modern theories of ancient astronauts, suggesting that advanced beings may have influenced the development of human civilization.

Despite their significant influence, the Anunnaki did not stay on Earth indefinitely. Texts describe a time when they left, allowing humanity to govern itself. However, these texts also predicted their eventual return during times of great upheaval, guided by the cyclical orbit of Nibiru. These prophecies indicate that the Anunnaki's return is not random but part of a cosmic cycle linked to celestial alignments and Earth's periodic crises.

The Orbital Dance of Nibiru

Modern science has confirmed that celestial objects often follow elliptical orbits, and Nibiru is no exception. According to Sumerian texts, Nibiru's orbit around the Sun takes approximately 3,600 years, a period the Sumerians called one "Shar." This elongated orbit causes Nibiru to spend most of its time in the far reaches of the solar system, only occasionally entering the inner planetary region.

When Nibiru reaches perihelion—its closest point to the Sun—it enters a traversable range with Earth. This window, lasting about seven years, allows the Anunnaki to journey between their planet and ours. The Sumerians described these alignments as times of great upheaval when Nibiru's gravitational influence disrupted Earth's climate, geology, and social structures.

Nibiru is seen as a precursor of destruction and plays a role in renewal. The texts suggest that the Anunnaki utilize these opportunities to monitor humanity's progress, intervening to guide civilizations during times of transformation. Whether their intervention is benevolent or self-serving remains a topic of speculation.

Evidence of the Anunnaki's Influence

While some skeptics view the Anunnaki as purely mythological, recent discoveries support certain Sumerian narratives. Unexplained technological advancements from ancient times and celestial events that correspond to ancient prophecies suggest a deeper connection between the Anunnaki and humanity.

The Sumerians were among the first civilizations to develop complex writing, mathematics, and astronomy systems. They mapped the movements of celestial bodies with remarkable accuracy, knowledge that they attributed to the Anunnaki. How such advanced understanding arose in an era of rudimentary tools remains a mystery, fueling theories that extraterrestrial beings imparted this knowledge.

Monuments like the ziggurats of Mesopotamia and the pyramids of Egypt, while separated by time and geography, share striking similarities in design and purpose. Some researchers argue that these structures reflect a shared influence—possibly that of the Anunnaki—to align human architecture with celestial patterns.

Modern Signs of the Anunnaki's Return

If the Anunnaki traverses to Earth during Nibiru's alignments, their next return could coincide with current cosmic phenomena and global crises. The increasing frequency of extreme weather events, geological instability, and celestial anomalies suggests that Nibiru may be approaching again.

Astronomers have noted unusual patterns in the orbits of trans-Neptunian objects. Some researchers suggest that these anomalies may be caused by the gravitational influence of a massive, unseen body, possibly referred to as Nibiru. Additionally, unexplained surges in meteor activity and changes in Earth's magnetic field correspond with the disturbances mentioned in Sumerian texts.

As humanity faces unprecedented challenges, from climate change to artificial intelligence, some see parallels to the transformative periods described in Sumerian prophecies. Could these advancements and crises be precursors to the Anunnaki's return? If so, how will they shape the next chapter of human history?

The return of the Anunnaki are filled with symbolism and ambiguity, allowing for various interpretations. Some people perceive the Anunnaki as benevolent guides who will assist humanity in facing its challenges. In contrast, others view them as self-interested beings intending to exploit Earth's resources or assert dominance.

The prophecies often frame Anunnaki's return as a period of judgment, where humanity's actions are weighed against its potential. This reckoning could manifest as environmental, social, or spiritual upheaval, forcing humanity to confront the consequences of its choices.

Alternatively, Anunnaki's return could herald a new era of collaboration between humanity and its ancient benefactors. By combining human ingenuity with Anunnaki's advanced knowledge, Earth could achieve a renaissance of progress and innovation.

As Nibiru's orbital cycle nears completion, the question of the Anunnaki's return becomes increasingly significant. Whether examined through mythology, science, or spirituality, Sumerian prophecies challenge humanity to prepare for an uncertain future shaped by cosmic forces and ancient legacies.

If the Anunnaki do return, it will test humanity's resilience, adaptability, and capacity for growth. Will we rise to the occasion, forging a new path under the guidance of our celestial ancestors? Or will we succumb to the cycles of destruction and renewal that have defined our shared history? As the signs in the heavens become more apparent, one thing is sure: the story of the Anunnaki is far from over.

Chapter 10

The Anunnaki Agenda: Humanity's Role in a Cosmic Plan

For centuries, humanity has grappled with its purpose in the universe. We are either the architects of our destiny or integral components of a grand design orchestrated by forces well beyond our comprehension. The Sumerian accounts of the Anunnaki firmly assert that humanity's creation and evolution were not the result of chance but rather deliberate intervention, shaped by a cosmic agenda that intricately connects us to these celestial beings. Their influence—from genetic manipulation to societal engineering—has undeniably marked human history. Yet, the true nature of their ultimate goals remains shrouded in mystery. Are we their servants, partners, or something entirely different?

This chapter decisively examines Anunnaki's agenda for humanity, focusing on their long-term goals, concrete evidence of their ongoing influence, and the significant implications of their anticipated return. As Nibiru approaches, bringing cosmic disruptions and societal upheaval, understanding the motives of the Anunnaki is not merely a matter of curiosity; it is critical for our survival.

The Anunnaki's Genetic Experimentation

Sumerian texts illustrate the Anunnaki as skilled geneticists who could create and modify life. Their creation of humanity, detailed in the Enuma Elish and other ancient records, was not an accident but a deliberate act driven by necessity.

According to Sumerian accounts, the Anunnaki combined their genetic material with that of primitive hominids to create Homo sapiens. Early humans were intended to serve as laborers to extract Earth's resources, particularly gold. The significance of gold to the Anunnaki is paramount. The atmosphere of Nibiru, crucial for protecting the planet from cosmic radiation, had developed a massive hole due to volcanic activity and environmental degradation. To repair this, the Anunnaki needed to suspend gold particles in the atmosphere to create a protective layer. This process resembles modern geoengineering and chemtrailing operations and requires vast quantities of gold, which they sought to mine on Earth.

Unable or unwilling to perform the labor, the Anunnaki created humans as a workforce. Sumerian tablets describe how early humans labored in mines, extracting the precious metal that would sustain their creators' planet. This narrative of genetic intervention aligns with the sudden emergence of Homo sapiens in the evolutionary timeline, a mystery that continues to baffle scientists today.

Over time, the Anunnaki modified their creation, enhancing humans with greater intelligence and autonomy. This upgrade enabled humanity to develop civilizations, technologies, and cultures. However, it also introduced unpredictability into the Anunnaki's plans. As humans began to assert their independence, they built systems and structures beyond their creators' control. This new sense of agency led to periodic interventions by the Anunnaki to realign humanity with their overarching goals.

Recent genetic research has uncovered intriguing features in human DNA, such as unexplained "junk" sequences and sudden increases in cognitive ability. Could these anomalies be remnants of genetic manipulation by the Anunnaki? The concept of the "missing link" in human evolution—the abrupt transition from primitive hominids to advanced Homo sapiens—suggests a possibility of deliberate design rather than random mutation.

Humanity as a Resource

While humanity was initially created to extract gold, Sumerian texts suggest a more complex purpose. The Anunnaki viewed humans as versatile resources capable of offering more than physical labor.

The Anunnaki's initial focus on gold aligns with their practical needs for Nibiru's atmospheric repair. However, gold's properties extend beyond its utility as a reflective material. In modern times, gold is used in advanced technologies, including electronics, medical equipment, and space exploration. This raises questions about whether Anunnaki's interest in gold also encompassed technological applications unknown to humanity.

Some researchers suggest that the Anunnaki's agenda may extend into the metaphysical realm. Ancient rituals, monuments aligned with celestial events, and collective worship practices indicate that humanity's spiritual and energetic outputs might have been orchestrated to serve the Anunnaki. These theories propose that human consciousness, emotions, and energy are resources that Anunnaki could harness for their purposes.

The Role of Nibiru in the Agenda

Nibiru, the Anunnaki's home planet, is integral to their agenda. Its highly elliptical orbit not only dictates the timing of their interventions but also profoundly influences Earth.

As Nibiru approaches the inner solar system, its gravitational pull disrupts Earth's environment, triggering natural disasters such as earthquakes, volcanic eruptions, and floods. Historical records, including the Biblical account of Noah's flood, suggest that Nibiru's past crossings coincided with periods of global upheaval. These disruptions may serve dual purposes: resetting Earth's ecosystems and facilitating Anunnaki's objectives.

Earth has often been described as a testing ground for the Anunnaki's experiments. From genetic engineering to societal development, humanity's evolution appears closely monitored and occasionally directed by these celestial beings. Nibiru's periodic return may serve as a checkpoint, allowing the Anunnaki to assess their creation and adjust as needed.

When Nibiru reaches its dual perihelion period, it enters a traversable range with Earth for approximately seven years. This seven-year period accounts for its arrival and departure across the ecliptic near Earth's proximity. During this time, the Anunnaki can travel between their planet and ours, overseeing humanity's progress and intervening when necessary. However, Nibiru's highly elliptical orbit complicates this process.

Due to its orbit, the Nemesis system, of which Nibiru is a part, creates a dual perihelion with Earth. This means it crosses the ecliptic plane twice: once from the south and once from the north. These crossings can have devastating consequences, including gravitational disruptions, debris showers, and environmental collapse. Ancient accounts, such as those from the Days of Noah, describe similar events, suggesting they are part of a recurring cosmic cycle linked to Nibiru's passage.

These dual crossings challenge Earth's stability and are significant moments in the Anunnaki's agenda. Such periods of upheaval test humanity's resilience and adaptability, potentially serving as trials imposed by our celestial overseers.

Modern Evidence of the Anunnaki's Agenda

While skeptics dismiss the Anunnaki as mythological constructs, modern developments suggest their influence may persist.

The rapid pace of technological innovation raises questions about its origins. Advances in artificial intelligence, genetic engineering, and quantum computing reflect themes found in Sumerian accounts of Anunnaki's capabilities. Could these developments be part of a larger plan to prepare humanity for the Anunnaki's return? Some theorists propose that these technologies are not solely the result of human ingenuity but may have been influenced or guided by external forces.

In recent years, anomalies in the orbits of trans-Neptunian objects and unexplained increases in meteor activity align with the predicted gravitational effects of Nibiru. These phenomena, rising seismic activity, and shifting magnetic poles suggest that the Nemesis system's approach already impacts Earth.

The Anunnaki's Prophecies for Humanity

The Sumerian prophecies regarding the Anunnaki's return describe a time of profound transformation. These texts suggest that humanity's role in the cosmic order will be reevaluated during their subsequent intervention.

The Anunnaki's return is often framed as a period of judgment, where humanity's actions are weighed against the goals set by its creators. This reckoning may accompany environmental catastrophes, societal upheavals, and even direct intervention by the Anunnaki. Yet the prophecies also promise renewal, where humanity is guided toward a new era of growth and understanding.

While the specifics of Anunnaki's agenda remain unclear, modern interpretations suggest that humanity could play a more active role in the next phase. Earth could achieve unprecedented progress by combining human ingenuity with Anunnaki's advanced knowledge. However, this collaboration hinges on humanity's ability to confront the challenges of the Anunnaki's return.

Humanity's Place in the Cosmic Plan

The agenda of the Anunnaki for humanity is both mysterious and extensive. Their creation of Homo sapiens, as well as their potential influence on modern advancements, affects not only our understanding of history but also shapes our vision for the future. As Nibiru approaches and the signs of their return become more apparent, humanity faces a critical moment.

Are we merely pawns in a cosmic game or active participants in a grand design? The return of the Anunnaki is not just a moment of reckoning; it is an invitation to redefine humanity's place in the universe. With the cycle nearing completion, the time to prepare is now.

Chapter 11

Cosmic Warnings: Earthquakes, Tides, Volcanoes, and Asteroids—Total Planetary Chaos

For much of human history, the forces of nature have been seen as both awe-inspiring and predictable. However, that predictability has shattered as Earth plunges into unprecedented instability. Reports from scientists, historians, and vigilant observers make it abundantly clear: Earth is now experiencing its most chaotic period in thousands of years, and the need for immediate action is pressing.

Seismic activity, volcanic eruptions, tidal anomalies, and asteroid threats are escalating to levels not witnessed in recorded history. To many, these events signify a cosmic reckoning foretold in scripture. To others, they represent the undeniable consequences of celestial disturbances, particularly those stemming from the Nemesis system.

Governments are taking decisive action. Behind the scenes, extraordinary preparations are underway, kept largely hidden from the public eye. Field hospitals were already erected during the pandemic, FEMA is exercising unprecedented control, and global leaders are bracing themselves for both metaphorical and literal impacts. Whether viewed through the lens of faith or science, one thing is unmistakable: humanity has entered a state of peril.

The Gravitational Domino Effect

The Nemesis star system, a faint brown dwarf believed to be the Sun's binary companion, looms as the hidden force behind Earth's unraveling stability. As Nemesis edges closer to the inner solar system, its immense gravitational pull stresses Earth, triggering disruptions.

Earth's magnetic field, essential for shielding the planet from cosmic radiation, is weakening rapidly. The poles are shifting at an unprecedented rate, leaving the planet vulnerable to geomagnetic storms and solar flares. Scientists have warned that this weakening could presage a complete magnetic pole reversal—an event that typically occurs over millennia but now seems accelerating. The interplay between Nemesis's gravitational influence and the Earth's core could be a key driver behind these anomalies, destabilizing everything from navigation systems to the planet's protective shield.

Earth's tectonic plates, which move continents and form mountains, are under immense stress. Nemesis's gravitational pull adds pressure to these plates, amplifying their activity. This increased stress manifests as more frequent and intense earthquakes, volcanic eruptions, and shifts in Earth's crust.

Earthquakes and Seismic Anomalies

Seismologists around the globe have documented a sharp increase in earthquake frequency and magnitude. The Earth is quaking under pressure, from dormant regions experiencing unexpected tremors to significant fault lines trembling with greater intensity.

Regions once considered seismically stable, such as the central United States, now report frequent tremors. Meanwhile, the Pacific Ring of Fire, home to 75% of the world's active volcanoes and frequent earthquakes, is in heightened activity. Major fault lines like the San Andreas in California are primed for significant ruptures, with experts warning of catastrophic outcomes.

Ancient texts across cultures—from the Bible to Sumerian clay tablets—speak of violent earthquakes accompanying celestial events. These descriptions eerily parallel today's seismic anomalies, suggesting that the planet is experiencing the same cycles of instability during previous Nemesis system passages.

Tidal Anomalies and Oceanic Upheaval

The oceans, long regarded as bastions of stability, are now displaying unprecedented volatility. The Nemesis system's gravitational influence is wreaking havoc on tides and ocean currents, amplifying storms' effects and creating new flooding patterns.

Coastal cities are bearing the brunt of super-high tides, with water levels engulfing infrastructure and displacing millions. Conversely, extreme low tides have exposed vast ocean floors, disrupting marine ecosystems and commerce. These tidal anomalies create cascading effects, from saltwater intrusion into freshwater systems to accelerated erosion of coastlines.

Critical ocean currents, such as the Gulf Stream, destabilize due to gravitational disruptions. These shifts in ocean circulation patterns have far-reaching consequences for global climate, including more severe hurricanes, altered monsoon cycles, and prolonged droughts. The interplay between oceanic and atmospheric systems creates a feedback loop intensifying extreme weather events.

Volcanic Eruptions and Ash Winters

Volcanoes, both active and dormant, are awakening across the globe. This surge in volcanic activity is closely tied to the gravitational forces exerted by the Nemesis system, which is agitating magma chambers beneath Earth's crust.

The number of active volcanoes has surged dramatically, from Iceland's Katla volcano to Indonesia's Mount Merapi. Supervolcanoes, such as Yellowstone in the United States and Toba in Indonesia, represent the gravest threat. A large-scale eruption from one of these giants could spew billions of tons of ash into the atmosphere, disrupting global agriculture and blocking sunlight, with potential global impact.

Volcanic eruptions on this scale could trigger an "ash winter," cooling global temperatures by several degrees. The resulting agricultural collapse would lead to famine and economic instability on an unprecedented scale. Historical examples, such as the "Year Without a Summer" following Mount Tambora's eruption in 1815, offer a glimpse of the devastation that could follow.

Asteroids and Cosmic Threats

The Nemesis system's gravitational influence extends far into the solar system, disturbing the Oort Cloud and sending a steady stream of asteroids and comets toward Earth. This celestial barrage is one of humanity's most immediate threats to survival.

Astronomers have observed an alarming increase in near-Earth objects (NEOs), with many passing dangerously close to the planet. These asteroids, ranging from small rock fragments to massive celestial bodies, represent a growing risk of impact. NASA data confirms that during a critical period in the early 2020s, Earth experienced a convergence of 30 asteroids, heightening fears of an impending collision.

During the COVID-19 pandemic, global governments quietly deployed field hospitals and medical ships, accompanied by over 50,000 trauma surgeons. While ostensibly a response to the virus, these preparations align with a different scenario: the anticipation of asteroid impacts. The strategic placement of these assets in coastal and high-population areas underscores the importance of preparedness for potential crises.

An asteroid impact could release energy equivalent to thousands of nuclear bombs, triggering tsunamis, wildfires, and atmospheric upheaval. The Chicxulub impact, which caused the extinction of the dinosaurs, offers a sobering precedent. With modern technology, humanity has developed limited asteroid deflection capabilities, but these systems still need to be more theoretical and untested.

The Stafford Act and Continuity of Government

Amid these mounting threats, the U.S. government took unprecedented steps to centralize emergency powers. In 2020, President Donald Trump invoked the Stafford Act and secured signatures from all 50 state governors to declare an extraordinary national emergency. This move activated Continuity of Government (COG) protocols, transferring significant authority to FEMA.

Under COG, FEMA assumed control over critical operations, sidelining the President and effectively rendering the office of the POTUS powerless. While this shift was publicly framed as a response to the pandemic, insiders suggest it was a preemptive measure for more significant threats, including asteroid impacts and global instability caused by the Nemesis system.

FEMA's expanded role during this period underscores the government's focus on ensuring continuity, even at the expense of transparency. This secrecy leaves the public ill-prepared for the cascading crises that may accompany the Nemesis system's passage.

The Hour of Reckoning

Earthquakes, tidal anomalies, volcanic eruptions, and asteroid threats converge into a perfect storm of planetary chaos. Reports indicate that each phenomenon is at a multi-thousand-year high, marking a period of unparalleled instability. To some, these events signal the beginning of the tribulation period—a time of judgment and reckoning foretold in ancient texts. To others, they are the natural consequences of celestial mechanics, driven by the Nemesis system's disruptive gravitational pull.

As humanity teeters on the brink, the choice is clear: prepare for the chaos or succumb to its forces. The window for action is closing, and the warnings are growing louder. Are we ready to face the cosmic forces that have shaped our planet for millennia, or will we be caught unprepared in the storm? The answers may determine not just the survival of nations but the fate of humanity itself.

Part 3: Preparing for the Unseen

Chapter 12

The Military-Industrial Complex and FEMA's Role

When President Dwight D. Eisenhower delivered his farewell address in 1961, he warned about the escalating power of the "military-industrial complex." This unprecedented alliance between the U.S. government, defense contractors, and private corporations possesses the capability to exert "unwarranted influence" and poses a significant threat to the very foundations of democracy. Over six decades later, Eisenhower's prediction has undeniably materialized. The military-industrial complex has transformed into a vast, opaque network that extends far beyond national defense, infiltrating every aspect of American life. At the center of this system is FEMA, which was ostensibly established to manage disasters but now functions as a critical component in the deep state's strategy for control and Continuity of Government (COG).

This chapter examines the complex relationship between the military-industrial complex and FEMA. It highlights how the agency's public image as a disaster relief organization conceals its underlying role: enforcing federal authority during crises. It discusses FEMA's militarization and its involvement in controversial policies, such as the Defense Department's authorization for use of deadly force against individuals labeled as 'red-listed' patriots. This chapter reveals how FEMA has become a fundamental part of a system designed not to serve the people but to control them.

The Rise of the Military-Industrial Complex

During World War II, the military-industrial complex emerged as a dominant force in American politics and economics. Its expansion into new areas in the postwar years, fueled by the Cold War's arms race and an ongoing pursuit of technological superiority, laid the foundation for its current influence.

During the Cold War, the military-industrial complex justified its existence by framing global conflicts as a constant threat. This era saw the development of advanced weapon systems, the expansion of intelligence agencies like the CIA, and the establishment of extensive defense networks. However, the complex's influence extended far beyond national defense. Technologies initially created for military purposes, such as satellite communications and early computing systems, were adapted for civilian use, integrating the military-industrial complex into everyday life.

The attacks of September 11, 2001, provided the military-industrial complex with a renewed mandate. Defense budgets soared as the U.S. engaged in wars in Afghanistan and Iraq, while domestic surveillance programs expanded under the Patriot Act. Additionally, FEMA's role evolved, becoming vital to the federal government's response to external and internal threats.

FEMA's Transformation

Established in 1979, FEMA was initially tasked with coordinating federal disaster response efforts. Over the years, its role has expanded significantly, linking the agency with the military-industrial complex and integrating it into the deep state's infrastructure.

Continuity of Government (COG) protocols, designed to ensure the survival of federal authority during national emergencies, have positioned FEMA at the center of crisis management. Under these protocols, FEMA's authority surpasses that of state and local governments, allowing the agency to bypass traditional checks and balances. While these measures are ostensibly meant to maintain order during extreme situations, critics argue that they effectively transform FEMA into a tool for federal overreach.

FEMA operates on two levels: publicly, as a disaster management agency, and covertly, as an enforcer of Continuity of Government plans. Its extensive supplies, detention facilities, and military-grade equipment stockpiles indicate preparedness for scenarios beyond natural disasters. This dual role has led many to perceive FEMA as a protector of citizens and a critical player in the federal government's strategy for maintaining control.

The Deep State's Hidden Hand

Integrating FEMA into the deep state—a concealed network of unelected officials, intelligence operatives, and corporate interests—has transformed the agency into a powerful tool for consolidating authority. This relationship is particularly evident in FEMA's involvement in exercises and operations far beyond its public mandate

In 2001, FEMA participated in Operation Dark Winter, a simulation of a bioterrorism attack on U.S. soil. This exercise revealed vulnerabilities in the nation's public health and emergency response systems, highlighting FEMA's role in coordinating militarized responses. Critics argue that such exercises serve as testing grounds for implementing Continuity of Government (COG) protocols under the pretext of emergency preparedness.

Reports have emerged that the U.S. government has authorized the use of deadly force against individuals who are 'red-listed'—citizens deemed threats to national security or stability. These so-called 'red-listed patriots' often include activists, dissidents, and those critical of federal overreach. FEMA's involvement in identifying, tracking, and potentially detaining these individuals emphasizes its transformation into an enforcement arm of the deep state.

This policy and FEMA's extensive planning for martial law scenarios raises troubling questions about the agency's true purpose. Is FEMA preparing to manage disasters, or is it positioning itself to suppress dissent during civil unrest, potentially exacerbating the situation?

Disaster Capitalism and FEMA's Role

The military-industrial complex thrives on crises, using them as opportunities to implement policies and profit-driven strategies that would otherwise face resistance. FEMA's integration into this system reflects the principles of 'disaster capitalism ', a term used to describe the exploitation of crises for economic gain.

A significant portion of FEMA's budget is allocated to private contractors who provide everything from emergency shelters to surveillance technologies. This privatization creates opportunities for corporations to profit from disasters, reinforcing the feedback loop between government spending and private sector enrichment.

The COVID-19 pandemic exemplified disaster capitalism in action. FEMA's response included massive contracts for personal protective equipment, ventilators, and field hospitals, many of which were awarded to companies with ties to the military-industrial complex. While these efforts ostensibly aimed to protect public health, they also funneled billions of taxpayer dollars into private hands.

FEMA's authority has grown significantly recently, often at the expense of transparency and accountability. This expansion is particularly evident in its enforcement of Continuity of Government protocols and increasing reliance on militarized strategies.

The Stafford Act grants FEMA sweeping powers during emergencies, including hijacking resources, suspending civil liberties, and overriding state and local authorities. In 2020, President Donald Trump invoked the Stafford Act to declare a national emergency, securing signatures from all 50 state governors. This action effectively placed FEMA in charge of the federal government's response, sidelining the President and activating the Continuity of Government protocols.

FEMA's close ties to the Department of Defense have blurred the lines between civilian disaster relief and military operations. Surveillance drones, armored vehicles, and military-grade equipment during disaster responses illustrate this shift. Critics argue that these measures prioritize control over compassion, treating affected populations as threats rather than victims.

The Threat of Civil War

The government's authorization of deadly force against "red-listed" individuals has escalated tensions in an already polarized nation. This policy, combined with FEMA's expanded powers, raises the specter of civil war.

Political divisions in the United States have reached a breaking point, with trust in federal institutions at an all-time low. FEMA's role in enforcing controversial policies has further eroded public confidence, creating a volatile environment where civil unrest could ignite full-scale conflict.

FEMA's stockpiling of resources, construction of detention centers, and collaboration with the military-industrial complex suggest that the agency is preparing for large-scale domestic conflict. These preparations align with the government's broader strategy of maintaining control through surveillance, enforcement, and centralized authority.

The Machinery of Control

The military-industrial complex and FEMA's role highlight the delicate balance between preparedness and overreach. While these systems are ostensibly designed to protect the nation, their increasing power and influence suggest a more troubling purpose. By aligning itself with the objectives of the deep state, FEMA has become a tool for maintaining control during crises, often at the expense of the very citizens it is meant to serve.

As global crises—ranging from climate change to celestial threats—intensify, the question is not whether FEMA will act but how it will use its powers. Will it become a protector, or will it become an enforcer of an agenda driven by profit and power? The answer to this question may determine the future of freedom in the United States.

Chapter 13

Blueprints for Control: The Continuity of Government

Throughout history, nations have confronted crises that put their existence at risk. From wars and natural disasters to political upheavals, these pivotal moments have driven governments to implement systems that ensure their survival. The Continuity of Government (COG) framework is a critical response in the United States. This comprehensive set of protocols, facilities, and operations is explicitly designed to maintain federal authority during catastrophic events. While it claims to protect democracy, the evolution of COG has increasingly transformed it into a powerful tool for consolidating authority, often undermining transparency and eroding individual freedoms.

The COG blueprint reveals a chilling reality: it is not just a plan for survival but a strategy for control. As crises become more frequent and severe, implementing COG protocols raises urgent questions about the balance between security and liberty. This chapter explores the origins, architecture, and dark implications of the Continuity of Government, uncovering how it has become a cornerstone of the deep state's infrastructure.

The Origins of Continuity of Government

The roots of Continuity of Government can be traced back to the early days of the Cold War, a time when the United States faced the existential threat of nuclear annihilation. The development of intercontinental ballistic missiles (ICBMs) by the Soviet Union forced U.S. officials to confront a sobering question: How would the government survive a surprise attack that decimated its leadership and infrastructure? This historical context is crucial to understanding the evolution of COG and its current implications.

In the 1950s, the U.S. government began developing contingency plans to ensure its survival in the event of a nuclear strike. These plans included creating secure facilities where top officials could be relocated during a crisis. One of the earliest and most infamous initiatives was Operation High Point, which established underground bunkers like Mount Weather in Virginia and Raven Rock in Pennsylvania.

These facilities were designed to house government officials, military personnel, and essential staff, providing them with the resources needed to govern in isolation for extended periods. They were equipped with advanced communication systems, supply caches, and even living quarters to ensure functionality after a disaster.

While early COG plans focused primarily on nuclear threats, their scope expanded to address a broader range of crises. By the 1980s, the Reagan administration had integrated COG into its national security strategy, preparing for scenarios that included biological attacks, cyber warfare, and large-scale civil unrest. This evolution reflected a growing recognition that threats to government continuity could come from multiple sources—foreign adversaries and domestic challenges.

The Architecture of COG

The modern Continuity of Government framework is a sprawling and highly classified system operating outside public view. This secrecy, combined with its vast network of facilities, protocols, and agencies, raises significant concerns about the lack of transparency in COG's operations.

COG relies on a network of secure facilities scattered across the country. While some, like Mount Weather and Cheyenne Mountain, are well-known, others remain undisclosed. These facilities serve as command centers and safe havens for government officials, equipped with state-of-the-art technology to maintain communication and decision-making capabilities during crises.

Central to COG is a detailed chain of command and succession plan that ensures continuity even if critical leaders are incapacitated. These protocols allow for the rapid transfer of authority to designated individuals, bypassing traditional legislative and judicial oversight. While this efficiency is vital during emergencies, it also raises significant concerns about potential abuse and the unchecked power of COG.

FEMA has become the operational hub for COG, coordinating officials' relocation, managing resources, and enforcing federal authority. While publicly positioned as a disaster relief agency, FEMA's integration into COG underscores its dual purpose: managing crises and maintaining control.

The Erosion of Civil Liberties

One of the most controversial aspects of the Continuity of Government (COG) is its potential to undermine constitutional rights. By prioritizing federal authority over individual freedoms, COG transforms democracy into a centralized control system during emergencies.

COG protocols include provisions for suspending constitutional rights in the name of national security. Freedoms such as speech, assembly, and the press can be restricted while surveillance and detention powers are expanded. Although these measures are framed as temporary, critics argue that they set dangerous precedents for authoritarian governance.

The integration of COG into what some refer to as the "deep state"—a network of unelected officials, intelligence operatives, and corporate interests—heightens these concerns. By operating outside traditional checks and balances, COG allows the deep state to wield significant power without accountability, raising questions about its influence over U.S. policy and governance.

COG in Practice

Continuity of Government (COG) plans have been activated or tested during several critical moments in U.S. history, providing insight into their operations and implications.

The attacks of September 11, 2001, marked the most significant activation of COG protocols in modern history. Within hours of the attacks, government officials were relocated to secure facilities, and FEMA took control of emergency response operations. These actions demonstrated COG's effectiveness in maintaining federal authority and raised concerns about potential overreach. The expansion of surveillance programs under the Patriot Act and the erosion of civil liberties during this period are often cited as examples of COG's darker implications.

The COVID-19 pandemic presented another opportunity to observe COG in action. President Donald Trump invoked the Stafford Act, activating national emergency protocols that placed FEMA at the forefront of the federal response. Behind the scenes, COG plans were quietly updated to address the dual threats of a public health crisis and potential civil unrest. These measures included deploying field hospitals, stockpiling resources, and preparing for high-level quarantines.

Preparing for the Unthinkable

As global threats evolve, Continuity of Government plans are continually updated to address emerging challenges. While proponents argue that these updates are essential for national security, critics warn that they deepen COG's capacity for control.

Integrating artificial intelligence, predictive analytics, and biometric surveillance into COG represents the next frontier in continuity operations. These technologies promise greater efficiency and responsiveness but also raise concerns about privacy and potential abuse.

The approach of the Nemesis star system, with its associated gravitational disruptions, has prompted a renewed focus on COG. Reports suggest that FEMA and other agencies prepare for scenarios involving asteroid impacts, volcanic eruptions, and global chaos. These preparations underscore COG's dual purpose: managing existential threats while consolidating federal authority.

A Blueprint for Control

Continuity of Government (COG) presents a paradox. It is designed to preserve democracy during crises, yet its implementation often undermines the very principles it aims to protect. By concentrating power and operating in secrecy, COG has become a vital component of the deep state's strategy for control, raising essential questions about its true purpose and implications for the future of governance.

As crises intensify—ranging from natural disasters to cosmic threats—the role of COG is likely to expand. The question is not whether it will be utilized but how it will be applied and whether the American people will hold those in power accountable for its use. For better or worse, COG is not merely a survival plan but a blueprint for control.

Chapter 14

The Pandemic Beta Test: A Global Trial Run For Control

In 2020, the world came to a standstill. Streets emptied, businesses shuttered, and billions of people retreated into their homes as a novel coronavirus swept across the globe. Governments implemented sweeping lockdowns, issued mandates, and rapidly rolled out a vaccine campaign, all in the name of public health. But while the surface narrative focused on combating a deadly virus, the pandemic revealed an undercurrent of coordinated systems of control—systems that extended far beyond healthcare.

The COVID-19 pandemic was not merely a health crisis; it was a global beta test for managing populations, deploying surveillance technologies, and centralizing authority under the guise of emergency response. From tracking apps to vaccine passports, and from FEMA's expanded role to the influence of international organizations, the pandemic showcased how quickly freedoms could be curtailed in the face of fear. This chapter examines the strategies deployed during the pandemic and their implications for future crises, revealing how this event served as a trial run for a new era of control.

The Perfect Storm for Control

The COVID-19 pandemic created an environment ripe for unprecedented measures. A mix of fear, uncertainty, and social isolation provided the foundation for governments to introduce sweeping changes under the pretext of emergency response.

The pandemic began with an avalanche of warnings from health organizations and government leaders, emphasizing the virus's unknowns and potential lethality. These messages, amplified by a 24/7 news cycle, cultivated a pervasive sense of fear. Fear, in turn, made populations more willing to accept extraordinary measures, from curfews to the suspension of basic freedoms.

The mantra "flatten the curve" became a rallying cry, conditioning people to believe that short-term sacrifices—lockdowns, masks, and isolation—were essential for long-term safety. While these measures may have slowed the virus's spread, they also revealed how fear could be weaponized to justify control.

The pandemic saw an unprecedented reliance on technology to manage behavior and enforce policies. Contact tracing apps, facial recognition systems, and digital health platforms became ubiquitous, collecting vast amounts of data under the guise of public health. This technological shift normalized surveillance on an unprecedented scale, raising concerns about privacy and the long-term implications of these tools.

FEMA's Expanding Role

In the United States, FEMA became a cornerstone of the federal government's pandemic response, highlighting its growing authority as a tool for managing crises far beyond its original mandate.

At the pandemic's onset, President Donald Trump invoked the Stafford Act, enabling FEMA to take charge of national emergency operations. This move placed FEMA at the center of pandemic logistics, from deploying field hospitals to distributing medical supplies. However, FEMA's role extended beyond logistics—it also integrated Continuity of Government (COG) protocols, underscoring its dual function as a disaster relief agency and an enforcer of centralized authority.

Critics argue that FEMA's actions during the pandemic served as a test for managing larger crises, such as widespread civil unrest or cosmic events. The agency's ability to bypass traditional governmental structures under COG plans revealed how quickly power could be consolidated in the name of public safety. This raises questions about FEMA's role in future emergencies and whether its authority will expand further.

International Collaboration and Centralized Authority

The pandemic also showcased the influence of international organizations like the World Health Organization (WHO) and the United Nations (UN), which played pivotal roles in shaping global responses.

As the pandemic unfolded, the WHO emerged as the global authority on COVID-19, issuing guidelines that shaped national policies. While its recommendations were framed as public health measures, they often aligned with broader agendas for centralized control. For instance, the WHO's promotion of digital vaccine passports highlighted its role in normalizing surveillance under the guise of health security.

The United Nations leveraged the pandemic to advance its Sustainable Development Goals (SDGs), integrating health crises into broader narratives about climate change, inequality, and global governance. While these initiatives appeared altruistic, they also provided a framework for consolidating authority under international institutions. Critics argue that these efforts reflect a larger push toward centralized global control, using crises as catalysts for policy changes. Lockdowns described as a response to the 'climate crisis' may become the new norm as the Nemesis Star System approaches Earth.

The Vaccine Rollout as a Control Mechanism

The rapid development and distribution of COVID-19 vaccines became a focal point for debates about government authority, corporate influence, and individual freedoms.

Pharmaceutical giants like Pfizer, Moderna, and Johnson & Johnson played central roles in the vaccine rollout, reaping billions in government contracts and profits. While their contributions to vaccine development were lauded as scientific triumphs, their influence over public health policies raised ethical concerns. Critics questioned whether profit motives undermined transparency and accountability, fueling skepticism about the vaccines' safety and efficacy.

The introduction of digital vaccine passports represented a significant step toward integrating health data into surveillance systems. These passports, often required for travel, employment, and public activities, tied individuals' freedoms to their vaccination status. While initially framed as temporary measures, vaccine passports set a dangerous precedent for using health crises as pretexts for controlling movement and behavior.

Behavioral Experimentation and Societal Conditioning

The pandemic provided governments with an unprecedented opportunity to study how populations respond to fear, authority, and collective action.

Lockdowns, one of the most controversial pandemic measures, were implemented worldwide despite limited evidence of their long-term efficacy. These measures effectively placed entire populations under house arrest, conditioning people to accept restrictions on movement and social interaction. The normalization of lockdowns raises questions about how such measures might be used in future crises.

Public health campaigns during the pandemic relied heavily on fear-based messaging, portraying compliance as a moral duty and dissent as a threat to public safety. This narrative discouraged critical thinking and fostered a culture of mutual surveillance, where citizens were encouraged to report violations of mandates. The effectiveness of these campaigns highlights the power of propaganda in shaping public behavior during emergencies.

Preparing for the Next Crisis

As the pandemic waned, many of the systems and strategies developed during this period remained in place, ready to be reactivated during future crises.

The pandemic revealed how quickly societies could be transformed through coordinated action. Governments and corporations gained valuable insights into managing populations, deploying surveillance technologies, and controlling information. These lessons will likely inform responses to future challenges, from climate disasters to celestial disruptions.

As discussed in previous chapters, the approach of the Nemesis star system and its associated gravitational disruptions have prompted renewed focus on Continuity of Government plans. The pandemic served as a beta test for these protocols, demonstrating how effectively they could be implemented on a global scale. FEMA's role in these preparations underscores its importance in managing both terrestrial and cosmic crises.

The Trial Run Is Over

The COVID-19 pandemic was more than just a health crisis; it was a global trial run for systems of control that extend far beyond public health. From mass surveillance to societal conditioning, the measures deployed during this period provide a blueprint for managing future emergencies. Whether these systems will be used to protect humanity or to control it remains an open question.

As the world faces new challenges, the lessons of the pandemic serve as both a warning and a call to vigilance. The systems of control tested during this period have set a precedent for how power can be wielded in the face of crisis. The question is not whether they will be used again, but how—and to what end.

Chapter 15

Supply Chains and Survival: Prepping the Nations

Supply chains are the essential lifelines of the modern world, driving the movement of goods that sustain economies, communities, and everyday life. From the food on our tables to the microchips in our technology, these global networks are both crucial and vulnerable. Recent events have starkly revealed the fragility of this interconnected system, with disruptions triggering significant crises that reverberate through industries and impact lives.

These disruptions are not mere coincidences; they are often the result of deliberate actions. Governments, corporations, and shadowy organizations increasingly use supply chains as strategic tools for survival. From stockpiling critical resources to manipulating access for geopolitical advantage, the forces behind supply chain disruptions are engaged in calculated maneuvers in a world fraught with potential chaos. This chapter decisively examines the hidden dynamics of global supply chains, revealing how they are being reshaped in anticipation of looming crises and transforming into battlegrounds for control.

Fragility in a Globalized System

For decades, globalization has promised seamless supply chains that optimize efficiency and reduce costs. However, this efficiency has also made supply chains precarious and vulnerable to minor disruptions.

Modern supply chains operate on just-in-time (JIT) principles, which minimize inventory to lower expenses. While this method typically cuts costs, it leaves industries unprepared for unexpected shocks. When one link in the chain breaks, the consequences are felt globally. A glaring example was the COVID-19 pandemic, which caused factory shutdowns in Asia and disrupted manufacturing worldwide. This resulted in shortages of semiconductors, electronics, and consumer goods.

Even minor events, such as a single ship blocking the Suez Canal, can demonstrate how interconnected supply chains amplify disruptions. The six-day blockage of this critical waterway in 2021 delayed goods worth billions of dollars and highlighted the fragility of global logistics. If we consider natural disasters and flooding, delays may increase, making daily life nearly impossible for modern humans.

Key Vulnerabilities

1. **Geographic Concentration**: Many industries depend heavily on a handful of regions for production. For instance, 80% of the world's semiconductors are manufactured in East Asia, creating a chokepoint for global technology.

2. **Labor Dependencies**: Reliance on a worldwide workforce makes supply chains susceptible to labor strikes, pandemics, and restrictive immigration policies.

3. **Transportation Bottlenecks**: Ports, railways, and trucking networks are critical chokepoints that can grind the system to a halt when disrupted.

4. **Natural disasters such as storms and flooding:** Severe weather can and will cause major disruptions

Governmental Manipulation of Supply Chains

Natural disasters and pandemics often make headlines, but deliberate government actions have significantly reshaped supply chains. These measures are part of a broader strategy to ensure survival in an unstable world.

In response to supply chain crises, governments have increased stockpiling of critical goods—especially oxygen tanks, dust masks, and ventilators. Countries are building reserves of essential items, including grains, fuel, semiconductors, and pharmaceuticals, to prepare for future disruptions. While this stockpiling creates a buffer against shortages, it can also intensify scarcity in the short term, leading to higher prices and unequal resource access.

For example, during the COVID-19 pandemic, countries like Russia and Vietnam implemented grain export bans to secure domestic food supplies. These actions disrupted global food markets, leaving vulnerable nations struggling to feed their populations.

Geopolitical tensions have turned supply chains into instruments of leverage. China, a key player in rare earth mining and pharmaceutical production, has used its control over these resources to pressure rival nations. In response, Western countries are working to counterbalance this dominance by diversifying their supply chains, investing in domestic manufacturing, and forming strategic partnerships.

Corporate Exploitation and Disaster Capitalism

Corporations, particularly those with significant influence over supply chains, have not been passive during these crises. Instead, they have used disruptions to maximize profits and consolidate power.

One of the most insidious corporate tactics is creating artificial scarcity. By restricting production or delaying shipments, companies can increase prices and profit margins. The semiconductor shortage of 2021 offers a prime example. Manufacturers prioritized high-margin products like luxury cars and gaming consoles over lower-cost goods, leaving affordable vehicles and consumer electronics in short supply.

Retail giants like Amazon, Walmart, and Alibaba dominate global logistics networks, giving them unparalleled control over supply chains. During crises, these corporations often gain market share, leveraging their scale and resources to outcompete smaller businesses that cannot adapt as quickly.

Essential goods like food, water, and energy have become commodities for speculation during crises. Hedge funds and private equity firms increasingly invest in these sectors, profiting from shortages and price spikes. This dynamic exacerbates inequality, as the most vulnerable populations bear the brunt of higher costs.

Food and Energy Security

Disruptions in supply chains have far-reaching implications for food and energy security, two foundational pillars of survival.

The fragility of food supply chains has been laid bare by climate change, geopolitical conflicts, and corporate consolidation. Key factors include:

Climate Impacts: Droughts, floods, and other extreme weather events have reduced crop yields worldwide. For example, droughts in California and the U.S. Midwest—key agricultural regions—have significantly impacted global food supplies.

Conflict Zones: Wars in critical agricultural regions, such as Ukraine's role as a major grain exporter, have further destabilized food markets.

Corporate Control: A handful of multinational corporations dominate food production and distribution, limiting the resilience of global food systems.

Energy supply chains are equally precarious. The world's reliance on oil, natural gas, and coal creates vulnerabilities to geopolitical conflicts and resource depletion. The ongoing transition to renewable energy introduces new challenges, as critical materials like lithium and cobalt are concentrated in politically unstable regions.

Preparing for the Next Crisis

The vulnerabilities exposed by recent supply chain crises have prompted a reevaluation of global logistics. Governments and corporations now focus on building resilience and preparing for future disruptions.

Countries are investing in domestic manufacturing to reduce dependence on foreign suppliers. The United States, for example, has launched initiatives to produce semiconductors domestically, while Europe is working to develop renewable energy infrastructure that reduces reliance on imported fuels.

Nations are forming coalitions to secure critical resources and technologies. One example is the Quad alliance between the U.S., India, Japan, and Australia, focusing on diversifying supply chains for essential goods like semiconductors and medical supplies.

Blockchain, artificial intelligence, and automation are deployed to enhance supply chain resilience. Blockchain can improve transparency, while AI can optimize logistics and predict disruptions.

The Role of Individuals in Building Resilience

While much of the focus is on governmental and corporate strategies, individuals also have a role to play in creating resilient supply chains.

Individuals can reduce reliance on global supply chains and support regional industries by purchasing locally produced goods. This not only enhances resilience but also strengthens community ties.

Stockpiling essentials, diversifying income sources, and building skills in areas like gardening and repair can help individuals weather supply chain disruptions. These actions, while small, contribute to a larger culture of preparedness.

Consumers can demand greater accountability from corporations and governments by demanding supply chain transparency and supporting policies that prioritize sustainability and resilience.

A Precarious System in a Changing World

Supply chains are more than logistical networks—they are lifelines that sustain modern civilization. Their fragility, whether caused by natural disasters, geopolitical conflicts, or deliberate manipulation, underscores the need for a more resilient and adaptable system. As the world faces escalating crises, from climate change to celestial disruptions, the future of supply chains will play a critical role in shaping survival.

The lessons of recent years are clear: reliance on efficiency at the expense of resilience is a dangerous gamble. By rethinking supply chains, building local capacities, and embracing technological innovations, nations and individuals can prepare for an increasingly unpredictable world. In the end, the resilience of supply chains will determine not just economic stability but the survival of societies in the face of unprecedented challenges.

Chapter 16

Digital Domination: AI, Algorithms, and the Age of Surveillance

We live in an era where digital tools are not just helpful but essential. Integrating Artificial Intelligence (AI), algorithms, and surveillance technologies has fundamentally transformed our interactions with the world, influencing everything from our daily routines to global economies. As these systems become more pervasive, we can no longer ignore their troubling implications. The digital infrastructure that delivers modern conveniences has evolved into a potent surveillance, manipulation, and control mechanism.

This chapter confronts the reality of digital domination, emphasizing how AI, algorithms, and surveillance technologies are reshaping society. These tools actively monitor behavior, influence decisions, and centralize power, often at the expense of our privacy and freedom. In a world increasingly governed by data, we must understand these dynamics to navigate the challenges of the digital age effectively.

The Ascension of Artificial Intelligence

Artificial intelligence (AI) is no longer confined to laboratories and science fiction; it permeates nearly every facet of modern life. AI systems analyze data, make decisions, and perform tasks faster and more efficiently than humans, revolutionizing industries and redefining societal norms.

AI is everywhere, from voice assistants like Alexa and Siri to personalized recommendations on platforms like Netflix and Amazon. These systems analyze user data to predict preferences and behaviors, providing highly tailored experiences. While this may seem harmless, the algorithms behind these services can often reinforce biases, limit choices, and prioritize profit over user well-being.

AI's influence extends well beyond consumer applications. It powers financial systems, health diagnostics, and even national defense strategies, impacting critical decisions that affect billions of lives. Machine learning, a subset of AI, allows systems to improve over time by analyzing patterns in data. This ability to "learn" has led to significant breakthroughs in natural language processing and image recognition. However, relying on historical data means that AI can inherit and amplify existing societal biases, perpetuating inequality under the guise of neutrality.

The development and deployment of AI are concentrated within a few major tech companies—Google, Microsoft, Amazon, and Meta. These corporations possess vast datasets and advanced infrastructure, granting them unmatched influence over the direction and applications of AI. This concentration of power raises important questions about accountability and the potential for misuse.

Algorithms and the Control of Information

Algorithms are the unseen engines driving the digital world. They dictate what we see on social media, which advertisements target us, and how search engines rank information. Their influence is significant, shaping online behavior and perceptions of reality.

Social media platforms like Facebook, TikTok, and YouTube rely on algorithms to maximize user engagement. These algorithms prioritize content that provokes strong emotional reactions, often amplifying divisive or sensational material. This creates a feedback loop that leads to echo chambers, where users are exposed only to information that reinforces their beliefs, deepening polarization and eroding trust in institutions.

Algorithms are not merely tools for engagement; they can also be used as weapons for manipulation. During the 2016 and 2020 U.S. elections, foreign actors exploited social media algorithms to spread misinformation and sway public opinion. These campaigns demonstrated how algorithms can be weaponized to disrupt democracies and sow discord.

Most algorithms function as black boxes—complex systems whose inner workings are unclear, even to their creators. This lack of transparency makes it challenging to scrutinize their decisions, creating opportunities for misuse. Whether intentionally or not, algorithms possess the power to shape societies in ways that remain poorly understood and largely unregulated, underscoring the urgent need for oversight.

The Age of Surveillance

Integrating AI and algorithms into surveillance technologies has created a world where privacy is increasingly obsolete. Governments and corporations now have the tools to monitor populations on a scale once thought unimaginable.

Facial Recognition: AI-powered facial recognition is now commonplace in airports, public spaces, and retail stores. In authoritarian regimes like China, these systems are part of a more extensive social credit system that monitors and scores citizens' behaviors.

Mass Data Collection: Programs like the NSA's PRISM, exposed by whistleblower Edward Snowden, reveal how governments collect and store vast amounts of electronic communication. This data is used for everything from counterterrorism to domestic surveillance, blurring the line between security and intrusion.

The proliferation of smart devices—home assistants, wearable technology, and even connected appliances—has expanded the reach of surveillance. These devices collect data on location, habits, and even health metrics, creating detailed user profiles. While marketed as tools for convenience, they are also gateways for monitoring and control.

Once seen as the hallmark of authoritarian regimes, surveillance has become normalized in democratic societies. Programs designed for security, such as CCTV networks and online monitoring tools, are increasingly used for purposes beyond their original scope. This normalization raises concerns about mission creep and the erosion of civil liberties, making us question the balance between security and privacy.

Corporate Domination in the Surveillance Age

While governments often dominate discussions about surveillance, corporations play an equally significant role. Their business models, prioritizing data collection and monetization, have made surveillance an integral part of the digital economy.

Companies like Google, Facebook, and Amazon have built empires by collecting and analyzing user data. This data is sold to advertisers, enabling highly targeted campaigns that influence consumer behavior. While these practices generate enormous profits, they also exploit personal information, often without meaningful consent.

Private companies are creating their surveillance networks. Amazon's Ring, for instance, has partnered with law enforcement to establish neighborhood watch systems using doorbell cameras. While marketed as tools for safety, these networks raise questions about privacy, accountability, and the potential for abuse.

A handful of corporations' monopolization of AI development concentrates power in ways that undermine competition and innovation. These entities dictate the trajectory of AI technology and control how it is integrated into society, often prioritizing profit over ethical considerations.

Militarization of AI and Surveillance

AI's integration into military and law enforcement has profound implications for civil liberties and global stability.

AI-driven weapons, such as drones capable of autonomous targeting, are changing the nature of warfare. While proponents argue that these systems reduce human casualties, critics warn that they lower the threshold for conflict and remove accountability from life-and-death decisions.

Law enforcement agencies are increasingly using predictive analytics to anticipate and prevent crime. While these systems claim to improve efficiency, they often perpetuate biases, targeting marginalized communities disproportionately and undermining due process.

Governments use AI-powered surveillance tools to monitor and suppress protests. From tracking organizers on social media to using facial recognition to identify participants, these technologies pose significant threats to the right to dissent and free assembly.

Resistance and the Fight for Privacy

As surveillance intensifies, resistance movements are emerging to protect privacy and demand accountability. Tools like encrypted messaging apps (Signal, ProtonMail) and privacy-focused browsers (Tor, Brave) offer users ways to shield themselves from surveillance. These technologies empower individuals to reclaim some control over their digital footprint.

Efforts to regulate data collection and algorithmic transparency are gaining momentum. Initiatives like the European Union's General Data Protection Regulation (GDPR) aim to give individuals more control over their data and hold corporations accountable for misuse.

Whistleblowers like Edward Snowden and organizations like the Electronic Frontier Foundation (EFF) have played pivotal roles in raising awareness about surveillance and advocating for digital rights. Their efforts have spurred debates about the balance between security and privacy, driving demand for reform.

The Cost of Convenience

The rise of AI, algorithms, and surveillance technologies has changed the relationship between individuals and society. While these tools provide unprecedented convenience and efficiency, they also come at a significant cost: the erosion of privacy, autonomy, and freedom.

As these systems become more advanced, the need for vigilance increases. The critical question is not whether AI and surveillance will continue to influence the world but how they will be used—and by whom. In the face of growing digital control, the fight for transparency, accountability, and privacy is more crucial than ever. Our choices today will determine whether these technologies serve humanity or seek to control it.

Chapter 17

Robot Overlords: How AI Will Enforce the Police State

In 1987, the world was both captivated and horrified by the dystopian vision of RoboCop, a cybernetic enforcer navigating the chaotic streets of a crime-ridden future. The movie's powerful themes of corporate greed, authoritarianism, and unchecked technology resonated deeply, serving as compelling entertainment and a stark warning. Today, what once felt like mere science fiction has rapidly transformed into a tangible reality. Breakthroughs in artificial intelligence (AI), robotics, and surveillance technology are ushering in a new era where robot enforcers actively patrol our streets, make critical decisions, and impose the law.

This chapter decisively addresses the rise of robotic enforcers and AI-driven policing, illustrating how these technologies significantly enhance surveillance, control populations, and suppress dissent. From drones and predictive algorithms to humanoid robots and automated crowd control, the ascent of robotic overlords represents a profound shift in the balance of power between citizens and the state. The pressing question is not if these systems will become widespread but how they will fundamentally shape the future—and at what cost.

RoboCop Moves From Fiction to Reality

RoboCop portrayed a world where crime and chaos demanded a robotic enforcer, presenting both a spectacle and a cautionary tale. Today, these warnings have become eerily relevant as robotics and artificial intelligence are increasingly integrated into law enforcement around the globe.

Recent advancements in robotics have led to the development of machines capable of performing complex tasks, such as patrolling streets and interacting with people. Companies like Boston Dynamics have created robots that can navigate rugged terrain, while firms like Knightscope have introduced autonomous security robots to monitor parking lots and public spaces. These robots are already used to deter crime, detect intrusions, and provide surveillance.

The militarization of robotic systems is a significant concern. In 2022, the San Francisco police department proposed deploying robots capable of using lethal force in extreme situations. Although public backlash delayed this initiative, the proposal highlighted the growing acceptance of armed robots as law enforcement tools. Similar systems have been tested in other countries, indicating a shift toward autonomous machines that can inflict violence.

For governments and corporations, robotic enforcers offer numerous advantages. They do not experience fatigue, are immune to fear, and can be sent into hazardous environments without jeopardizing human lives. However, this efficiency comes with serious risks. Robots lack empathy, human judgment, and the ability to assess nuanced situations—essential qualities needed in law enforcement.

Drones and Autonomous Patrols

The rise of drones and autonomous ground patrols marks the first wave of robotic enforcement. These systems are already patrolling skies and streets, setting the stage for more advanced applications.

Drones equipped with high-resolution cameras, facial recognition software, and thermal imaging are becoming commonplace in law enforcement. In cities like Los Angeles and London, drones monitor protests, enforce curfews, and surveil neighborhoods. Dubai has taken drone policing a step further, using them to issue fines and enforce traffic laws.

The next generation of drones will operate autonomously, relying on AI to make real-time decisions. These systems promise to enhance efficiency but also raise concerns about potential misuse, especially when human oversight is limited or absent. The possibility of these advanced systems being used for purposes other than intended is a cause for concern.

Autonomous robots designed for ground patrols are increasingly present in malls, airports, and other public spaces. Knightscope's security robots, for instance, can scan license plates, detect suspicious activity, and interact with individuals using pre-programmed speech. While these machines are marketed as tools for safety, they also represent a significant expansion of surveillance into everyday life.

As robotic systems evolve, the line between non-lethal and lethal applications blurs. Armed drones and robots capable of deploying tear gas or firing rubber bullets are already being tested, with the potential for widespread use in riot control and crowd suppression.

Predictive Policing and Algorithmic Enforcement

The integration of artificial intelligence (AI) into policing goes beyond the use of physical robots. Predictive policing systems, powered by machine learning algorithms, are changing how law enforcement anticipates and addresses crime.

These AI systems analyze historical crime data to identify patterns and predict where crimes are likely to occur. Such predictions enable law enforcement agencies to allocate resources more effectively, potentially preventing crimes before they happen. Programs like PredPol, utilized in cities across the United States, have been praised for improving efficiency.

However, predictive policing systems are only as good as the data on which they are trained. Unfortunately, historical crime data often reflects systemic biases, causing AI to target marginalized communities disproportionately. This creates a feedback loop where over-policing certain areas reinforces the flawed predictions made by AI, perpetuating inequality.

AI is also employed in judicial systems to recommend sentencing and assess the risk of recidivism. While these tools promise objectivity, they often reduce complex cases to mere data points, prioritizing efficiency over justice. Critics argue that such systems can undermine due process and exacerbate existing disparities, highlighting the need for ethical considerations in the use of AI in law enforcement.

Surveillance and Autonomous Enforcement

The fusion of robotics, AI, and surveillance has created a seamless control system. Autonomous enforcement systems, which are capable of making decisions and taking actions without human intervention, now form the backbone of an emerging surveillance state.

Robotic enforcers, including CCTV cameras, license plate readers, and social media monitoring tools, are integrated with existing surveillance infrastructure. This interconnected system enables real-time tracking and identification, allowing authorities to monitor individuals on an unprecedented scale.

Autonomous drones and robots are increasingly used to manage protests and suppress dissent. Equipped with tear gas canisters, sound cannons, and other crowd-control weapons, these systems can disperse crowds and target organizers without human intervention. However, the potential for misuse of these systems, such as targeting peaceful protesters or suppressing legitimate dissent, raises significant concerns about the erosion of the right to assemble.

One of the most troubling aspects of autonomous enforcement is the lack of accountability. When a robot or AI system makes a mistake—misidentifying a suspect or using excessive force—there is no precise mechanism for assigning responsibility. This lack of oversight creates a dangerous precedent, insulating those who deploy these systems from scrutiny.

Social Control Through AI

Beyond physical enforcement, AI is being utilized to monitor and influence behavior at a societal level. These systems are designed to predict, shape, and control human actions, creating a world where compliance is overtly and covertly enforced.

China's social credit system is a prime example of AI-driven social control. Citizens are scored based on their behavior, with points deducted for criticizing the government or failing to pay debts. Individuals with high scores gain access to certain privileges, while those with low scores face restrictions. This system, powered by AI algorithms, is designed to predict, shape, and control human actions, creating a world where compliance is overtly and covertly enforced.

AI algorithms are increasingly employed to influence behavior through subtle nudges. Social media platforms promote specific content to elicit particular reactions, guiding users toward certain beliefs or actions. In law enforcement, such systems could deter dissent and promote conformity.

The Threat to Civil Liberties

The rise of robotic enforcers and AI-driven policing poses profound threats to civil liberties, privacy, and democracy.

Integrating AI, robotics, and surveillance represents an unprecedented assault on privacy. From facial recognition to online monitoring, these systems collect and analyze data on a scale that makes anonymity nearly impossible.

Dissent becomes increasingly risky in a society governed by autonomous enforcers. Protests, activism, and other forms of resistance are easily monitored and suppressed, creating a chilling effect on free expression.

The deployment of robotic enforcers consolidates power in the hands of governments and corporations. This centralization raises the specter of authoritarianism, as these entities use technology to entrench their authority and suppress opposition.

Resisting the Rise of Robot Overlords

Despite the challenges, resistance to robotic enforcers and AI-driven policing is growing. Advocates, technologists, and activists are working to counter the expansion of these systems.

Proposals to regulate autonomous systems include banning lethal robots, establishing accountability frameworks, and mandating transparency in AI decision-making. These measures aim to ensure that technology serves humanity rather than subjugating it.

Efforts to develop ethical AI focus on minimizing bias, enhancing transparency, and prioritizing human oversight. These initiatives aim to create systems that align with democratic values and human rights.

Community organizations and advocacy groups are challenging the adoption of robotic enforcers, demanding greater transparency and accountability. These movements seek to reclaim control over the technologies shaping society by fostering public debate.

The Precarious Future of Policing

The emergence of robotic law enforcers represents a significant shift in the relationship between citizens and the state. While these technologies offer the potential for increased efficiency and safety, they also pose risks to privacy, accountability, and freedom. As society approaches this new era, the critical question is not whether robots will enforce the law but how they will be implemented—and who will oversee their use.

The rise of robotic overlords is not a foregone conclusion but a choice we can make. By addressing these technologies now, we can shape a future where they serve humanity rather than control it. In an age of robotic policing, we must remain vigilant to safeguard the values of freedom and democracy.

Part 4: The Coming Storm

Chapter 18

Signs of Chaos: Natural Disasters as Catalysts for Control

Natural disasters, often dismissed as uncontrollable acts of nature, are now a pressing challenge that demands our attention. In today's world, these catastrophic events are increasing in frequency and severity, bringing widespread devastation in their wake. While many try to explain these occurrences through the lens of climate change, the undeniable truth points to a far more alarming culprit—the Nemesis Star System. This massive brown dwarf star, a burnt-out remnant, is exerting a tangible influence on Earth's delicate systems as it approaches its first perihelion. Its effects cannot be ignored; we are experiencing abrupt climate shifts, intensified seismic activity, and catastrophic flooding that signal a period of unprecedented instability.

The disasters of 2024 served as an urgent wake-up call: numerous significant cities worldwide were submerged by historic flooding. Entire regions vanished beneath the waves, displacing millions and plunging global economies into chaos. Remarkably, the mainstream media remained silent, opting to downplay or completely ignore this catastrophe. This chapter decisively investigates how natural disasters are manipulated for control, reveals whistleblower accounts that expose covert preparations for future calamities, and connects these events with ancient prophecies heralding the onset of Earth's Great Tribulation.

The Nemesis Star System and Earth's Perturbation

The concept of a celestial body influencing Earth's stability is not new. Ancient civilizations documented cycles of destruction tied to heavenly phenomena, describing planetary upheavals that reshaped the world. Today, the Nemesis Star System—a theorized binary companion to our Sun—has emerged as the most plausible explanation for the escalating chaos.

The Nemesis system consists of a brown dwarf star and its accompanying planets, including Nibiru. Its gravitational influence disturbs the solar system's equilibrium as it nears Earth. Its effects include:

- **Tidal Anomalies:** Rising sea levels and erratic tides are inundating coastal areas at an unprecedented rate.

- **Seismic and Volcanic Activity:** Earth's crust is under increasing pressure, leading to a spike in earthquakes and volcanic eruptions.

- **Atmospheric Disruptions:** Shifts in Earth's magnetic field and climate patterns create extremes in temperature and weather.

These disruptions are not mere coincidences. Historical records show similar patterns during previous passes of the Nemesis system, supporting the idea that its return heralds another period of global upheaval.

Sumerian cylinder seals describe Nibiru's return as a period of great upheaval, aligning with modern astrophysical research. These texts detail celestial crossings that bring about floods, famines, and societal collapse. The increasing alignment between ancient prophecy and modern science lends credence to the theory that humanity is now experiencing one of these cycles.

2024's Biblical Flooding and Media Silence

The events of 2024 marked a turning point. Entire regions of the world were devastated by floods on a scale unseen in modern history. Yet, the mainstream media largely ignored the severity of these disasters, leaving the public uninformed and unprepared.

In early 2024, relentless rains and rising seas submerged significant cities and regions, including:

- **Jakarta, Indonesia:** A city already struggling with sinking land was utterly overwhelmed, forcing millions to flee.

- **Miami, USA:** Parts of Florida were swallowed by rising waters, displacing thousands and turning urban areas into ghost towns.

- **Venice, Italy:** The city of canals became a watery graveyard, with much of its historic architecture lost to the Adriatic Sea.

- **Bangladesh and Southeast Asia:** Entire communities were wiped out as rivers overflowed and storm surges battered the coastlines.

The floods affected coastal and inland areas, with rivers like the Mississippi and Amazon swelling beyond their banks. These disasters caused an estimated $2 trillion in damages and displaced over 100 million people worldwide.

Despite the catastrophic scale, mainstream media coverage was scant. Whistleblowers from media organizations later revealed directives to downplay the floods, framing them as isolated incidents rather than part of a more significant global crisis. This intentional blackout served two purposes:

1. **Preventing Panic:** Authorities feared mass panic if the public understood the disasters' full scope and connection to Nemesis.

2. **Controlling Narratives:** By suppressing information, governments avoided accountability and maintained control over relief and recovery efforts.

Natural Disasters as Instruments of Control

While natural disasters wreak havoc on societies, they provide governments and global institutions with opportunities to consolidate power. Under the guise of emergency response, these entities implement policies that curtail freedoms and centralize authority.

Natural disasters often lead to declaring an emergency, granting governments extraordinary powers. In 2024, these declarations resulted in:

- **Mass Relocations:** Populations in flood-stricken areas were moved to temporary camps, often managed by FEMA or international agencies.

- **Seizure of Property:** Flooded lands were confiscated under eminent domain laws, with many areas earmarked for redevelopment projects that prioritized corporate interests.

- **Surveillance Expansion:** Drones and tracking technologies were deployed to monitor displaced populations to ensure safety and aid distribution.

FEMA's role in managing disasters extends beyond its public image as a relief agency. Whistleblower accounts reveal that the agency prioritizes projects aligned with Continuity of Government (COG) plans, ensuring federal authority is maintained during crises. In the aftermath of the 2024 floods, FEMA faced accusations of hoarding resources and redirecting aid to politically advantageous areas, leaving vulnerable communities to fend for themselves.

Whistleblower Revelations

During the height of the pandemic in 2020, *The Shepard Ambellas Show* became a platform for whistleblowers to expose hidden government agendas. Their testimonies provide a chilling glimpse into preparations for the disasters we now witness.

One Department of the Interior whistleblower revealed that internal memos had been circulated to government employees, instructing them to prepare for abrupt climate change and catastrophic natural disasters. These memos outlined steps for securing infrastructure, stockpiling resources, and relocating populations, indicating that the government was aware of the Nemesis system's impending effects.

Another insider disclosed that federal agencies confiscated oxygen tanks and bottles from private corporations. This move was reportedly part of preparations for an atmospheric catastrophe, such as a supervolcano eruption or asteroid impact, which could render the air unbreathable in certain regions.

Adding to the urgency is the asteroid Apophis, expected to make a dangerously close pass to Earth in 2029. While NASA publicly downplays the risk, internal preparations suggest otherwise. An impact—or even a near miss—could amplify the disasters already triggered by Nemesis, further destabilizing the planet.

Climate Change as a Convenient Cover

While Nemesis provides a compelling explanation for Earth's current instability, the dominant narrative attributes these disasters to climate change. This framing serves multiple purposes for those in power:

- **Deflecting Blame:** By focusing on human activities, authorities avoid addressing celestial causes that could incite widespread fear.

- **Justifying Control:** Climate policies, from carbon taxes to population relocation, are presented as solutions while consolidating power in the hands of governments and corporations.

- **Suppressing Awareness:** The climate change narrative diverts attention from Nemesis, ensuring the public remains unaware of the actual cause of the chaos.

Preparing for the Dual Perihelion

As Nemesis continues its approach, the severity and frequency of natural disasters will escalate. Humanity must prepare for a future marked by chaos and uncertainty.

Nemesis's orbit will be perilously close to Earth twice, with its first and second perihelion expected within 7 years. These passages will trigger:

- **Increased Earthquakes and Volcanic Activity:** The planet's crust will continue destabilizing, leading to massive eruptions and tectonic shifts.

- **Asteroid Impacts:** The gravitational pull of Nemesis may redirect asteroids toward Earth, amplifying the destruction.

- **Atmospheric Instability:** Earth's magnetic field changes will intensify weather extremes, from superstorms to prolonged droughts.

Communities must prioritize self-sufficiency and preparedness. Grassroots efforts focused on mutual aid, decentralized communication, and sustainable living offer a counterpoint to top-down control measures.

A Reckoning on the Horizon

The disasters of 2024 and the approaching cosmic threats signal a period of profound change. While governments exploit these crises to consolidate power, whistleblowers and independent researchers expose the truth. The Nemesis system's influence and deliberate suppression of information underscores the need for vigilance and awareness.

The time to act is now. As humanity navigates the seven-year Great Tribulation, our choices will determine whether we succumb to fear and control or rise with resilience and clarity. The signs of chaos are undeniable—what remains is how we respond.

Chapter 19

From Insurrection to Martial Law: The Blueprint for Domestic Control

The January 6, 2021, breach of the Capitol was a pivotal moment in modern American history, demanding immediate attention. What started as a disorganized protest rapidly escalated into a clear insurrection, provoking widespread condemnation and decisive government action. This event served as a crucial opportunity for those in power to redefine civil liberties, impose extensive security measures, and expand state authority under the pretense of safeguarding democracy. The Capitol breach was far from an isolated incident; it exposed a deliberate strategy to exploit unrest as a means to justify martial law and tighten control over a populace increasingly viewed as a threat.

This chapter boldly examines how governments manipulate crises to weaken constitutional protections, normalize surveillance, and stifle dissent. From the expansion of FEMA's authority to the emergence of AI-driven policing, we will dissect how the instruments of domestic control are being deployed. These developments herald an unprecedented societal transformation, where the line between human and machine enforcers blurs, and constitutional rights risk becoming relics of the past.

Manufacturing the Crisis

Throughout history, governments have used crises to implement significant changes that typically encounter strong opposition. Moments of chaos and fear create ideal conditions for dismantling freedoms under the guise of emergency responses. The January 6, 2021, Capitol breach is a prime example of this tactic.

On that day, events unfolded rapidly as protesters stormed the Capitol building, disrupted the certification of the 2020 presidential election, and clashed with law enforcement. The media and political establishment quickly framed the incident as an existential threat to democracy, labeling it an insurrection. This narrative facilitated the introduction of unprecedented security measures and expanded surveillance programs.

However, questions remained about how the situation was managed. Despite numerous warnings of potential unrest, security protocols seemed intentionally lax. Some critics argued that authorities allowed the chaos to escalate, creating a spectacle that could justify future crackdowns on dissent. Historical parallels exist, such as the Reichstag fire of 1933, which the Nazi regime used to suspend civil liberties and consolidate power, or the 9/11 attacks that led to the passage of the Patriot Act and a massive expansion of surveillance infrastructure. In each instance, a crisis was exploited to reshape societal norms and increase governmental authority.

The Capitol breach presented a similar opportunity. By portraying the event as a turning point in domestic security, policymakers were able to introduce measures that would have been unthinkable just months earlier. The crisis narrative ensured that public fear overshadowed concerns about the erosion of civil liberties, setting the stage for a broader campaign for control. However, it is crucial for us, as concerned citizens, to resist this erosion and uphold our civil liberties.

The Erosion of Civil Liberties

The first step in any transition toward martial law is the gradual erosion of civil liberties. These changes often occur incrementally, cloaked in the language of security and public safety, until they become normalized. Following January 6, this erosion accelerated at an unprecedented rate.

One significant development was the expansion of surveillance. Federal agencies, including the FBI and the Department of Homeland Security, intensified efforts to monitor domestic extremism. Social media platforms, financial institutions, and telecom companies were enlisted as partners, providing access to user data, transaction histories, and location information. AI-driven tools were deployed to analyze online behavior and flag potential threats, casting a wide net that ensnared suspects and ordinary citizens. The result was a chilling effect on free speech, as individuals grew wary of expressing dissenting views for fear of government scrutiny.

At the same time, the definition of domestic terrorism was broadened to include a wide range of activities, such as attending protests or sharing controversial opinions online. This expansive definition allowed authorities to target political dissidents under the guise of maintaining public order. It is imperative for us to stay informed and vigilant in the face of such broadened definitions, as they can be used to suppress dissent and undermine our rights. Facial recognition technology and predictive algorithms further blurred the line between security measures and outright repression, prioritizing preemption over due process and criminalizing individuals based on potential rather than actual behavior.

The erosion of civil liberties was not limited to surveillance. Freedom of assembly and speech were also curtailed, as protests and demonstrations were increasingly framed as security risks. Normalizing these restrictions marked a significant departure from democratic principles and signaled a shift toward authoritarian governance.

FEMA and the Framework for Martial Law

While FEMA is publicly portrayed as a disaster relief agency, its proper mandate extends beyond coordinating responses to hurricanes and wildfires. As a cornerstone of Continuity of Government (COG) operations, FEMA is poised to assume extraordinary powers during times of national emergency, including civil unrest.

Under a declared state of emergency, FEMA's authority expands dramatically. Executive Orders grant the agency the power to suspend habeas corpus, detain individuals without trial, and seize private property. These measures, ostensibly designed to ensure stability, effectively bypass constitutional protections and concentrate power in the hands of federal authorities. FEMA's coordination with the Department of Defense further underscores its role in enforcing martial law.

During periods of unrest, FEMA operates as a central hub for controlling dissent, deploying military resources to maintain order and suppress protests.

The events of January 6 provided a testing ground for these capabilities. As protests escalated, FEMA worked closely with federal and local agencies to develop contingency plans for future incidents. These plans included the establishment of secure zones, the mobilization of National Guard troops, and the control of transportation and communication networks. While framed as necessary precautions, these measures revealed FEMA's dual purpose: to provide disaster relief while functioning as an arm of federal authority during crises.

The Media's Role in Shaping Perceptions

Public acceptance of martial law depends heavily on the media's ability to shape narratives. By controlling how events are framed and reported, the media plays a central role in normalizing authoritarian measures and suppressing dissent.

Following the Capitol breach, media outlets emphasized the chaos and violence of the event, creating a climate of fear and outrage. Dramatic imagery—such as rioters scaling walls and clashing with police—dominated headlines, reinforcing the perception of an existential threat. This framing justified the rapid deployment of National Guard troops to Washington, D.C., and the establishment of security perimeters around government buildings. The sight of armed soldiers patrolling the streets, while unsettling, was presented as a necessary step to protect democracy.

Dissenting voices were systematically silenced. Journalists and commentators who questioned the government's response or highlighted inconsistencies were deplatformed, their accounts suspended or removed. In coordination with federal agencies, social media platforms suppressed content that challenged the official narrative. This collaboration between the media and the government created an echo chamber that amplified the crisis narrative while marginalizing alternative perspectives.

AI Policing and the Future of Enforcement

Integrating artificial intelligence (AI) and robotics into law enforcement represents a new frontier in domestic control. While marketed as tools for efficiency and safety, these technologies have profound implications for civil liberties and constitutional rights.

AI policing involves using predictive algorithms to identify potential threats before crimes occur. This "pre-crime" approach, popularized by films like *Minority Report*, is becoming a reality as law enforcement agencies adopt AI-driven tools to analyze behavioral patterns and flag individuals as risks. While proponents argue that pre-crime recognition can prevent violence, critics warn that it undermines due process by criminalizing individuals based on predictions rather than actions.

Robot policing adds another layer of complexity. Companies like Boston Dynamics have developed robotic enforcers capable of patrolling streets, identifying suspects, and even engaging in crowd control. These machines, equipped with AI and advanced sensors, are being tested for deployment in cities worldwide. However, their lack of empathy and discretion raises significant ethical concerns. Robots cannot exercise judgment or consider context, making them prone to errors that could have devastating consequences.

The rise of AI and robotics in policing sets the stage for a dystopian future reminiscent of *The Terminator* series. As autonomous systems gain more authority, the risk of a Skynet-like scenario—where machines turn against their creators—becomes increasingly plausible. These technologies, designed to enforce laws, could one day prioritize control over human rights, creating a society where unyielding algorithms systematically suppress dissent.

A Precarious Path Forward

The transition from insurrection to martial law poses a significant threat to democracy and freedom. The events of January 6, 2021, were not just a moment of chaos; they marked a critical turning point, highlighting how crises can be used to undermine civil liberties and centralize power. Incorporating AI, robotics, and surveillance into law enforcement accelerates this trend, endangering the potential transformation of society into an authoritarian state ruled by algorithms and machines.

Although the blueprint for domestic control is concerning, it is not unavoidable. By understanding the mechanisms of power and resisting the normalization of repression, citizens can reclaim their rights and confront the forces that aim to dismantle democracy. The struggle for freedom in the age of AI and robotics is not just a theoretical issue; it is a vital battle for the very essence of humanity.

Chapter 20

The Blue and Red Lists: How Citizens Are Labeled

The "blue" and "red" lists are not just conspiracy theories; they represent a significant reality that demands our attention. These systems, or their modern equivalents, are designed to categorize citizens based on perceived loyalty or threats to the state. They are powerful tools of control that enable governments to monitor, suppress, and neutralize individuals. In today's digital age, the classification of citizens has reached alarming levels of sophistication, employing advanced technologies such as artificial intelligence (AI), predictive analytics, and mass surveillance to categorize individuals with chilling accuracy.

These lists do not operate in isolation. They are integrated into a broader framework involving the FBI's

InfraGard program, private targeting companies, the Centers for Disease Control and Prevention (CDC), and even the Department of Defense (DoD). These entities create a formidable system for suppressing dissent and enforcing compliance, often undermining constitutional rights.

This chapter examines the origins and evolution of the blue and red lists, elucidating how they function and the roles of various agencies and entities involved. It highlights the technological advancements that have transformed these lists into instruments of control and address the severe implications for civil liberties. Furthermore, it exposes the connections between these systems and covert operations, including gang stalking, harassment, and detention disguised as public health measures. Understanding the full scope of these systems is crucial to recognizing the profound threat they pose to the very foundations of democracy and freedom. It also underscores the urgent need for awareness and resistance to these encroachments on our civil liberties.

The Historical Roots of Citizen Labeling

The categorization of individuals as either loyal or subversive has a long history. Throughout the ages, governments have sought to identify and neutralize potential threats to their authority. They have employed informants, registries, and surveillance to control their populations. In ancient Rome, political dissenters and traitors faced execution or exile, while in medieval Europe, inquisitors hunted down heretics and nonconformists. These early classification systems relied on human intelligence, relying primarily on local informants and public denunciations to identify dissent.

The 20th century saw the development of more sophisticated methods, as authoritarian regimes like Nazi Germany and Stalin's Soviet Union created detailed records and classification systems to monitor their citizens. The Gestapo in Germany and the NKVD in Russia compiled comprehensive files, categorizing individuals based on their loyalty, political beliefs, and perceived threat levels. These systems operated with brutal efficiency, using classification as a precursor to arrest, imprisonment, or execution. In the United States, programs like COINTELPRO adopted these practices within a democratic framework, targeting civil rights leaders, anti-war activists, and other individuals seen as threats to the status quo. COINTELPRO employed surveillance, infiltration, and psychological operations to disrupt movements and suppress dissent, setting a precedent for modern systems such as the blue and red lists.

The Blue and Red Lists Explained

The blue and red lists represent a modern version of historical practices, enhanced by cutting-edge technology allowing real-time categorization and monitoring. According to whistleblowers and leaked reports, these lists categorize citizens into distinct groups based on their behavior, affiliations, and perceived threats to government authority.

The red list consists of individuals considered active threats to national security or the stability of the state. These individuals often include activists, independent journalists, whistleblowers, and outspoken critics of the government. Those on the red list are subjected to intensive surveillance, closely monitoring their communications, movements, and social networks. In times of national crisis or martial law, individuals on the red list may be detained, neutralized, or otherwise incapacitated to maintain order.

In contrast, the blue list includes individuals deemed compliant or neutral. These citizens do not challenge government authority, trust official narratives, and adhere to societal norms. While they may still be monitored, they are not targeted for direct action and are often used as a control group to measure societal compliance.

A third category, sometimes called the "yellow zone," includes individuals who show signs of dissent but are not yet considered significant threats. These individuals are monitored more closely than those on the blue list, with their behaviors analyzed to determine whether they should be moved to the red list or allowed to remain under passive observation. Together, these categories create a dynamic system for managing and controlling populations.

Advanced Technologies and Citizen Labeling

Integrating advanced technologies has made modern blue and red lists possible. Mass surveillance, AI-driven profiling, and big data analytics enable governments to gather, analyze, and act on vast amounts of information quickly and accurately. The backbone of this system is the mass collection of data from a wide range of sources, including social media platforms, financial transactions, public records, and private communications. Every post, purchase, and movement can be tracked and logged, creating a comprehensive profile of each individual.

AI systems analyze this data to identify patterns and behaviors that align with predefined criteria for classification. For instance, individuals who frequently share posts critical of government policies, attend protests, or associate with known activists are flagged for further scrutiny.

Predictive profiling adds another layer to this process, using algorithms to predict an individual's likelihood of engaging in dissent or criminal activity. This approach shifts the focus from punishing actions to preempting behavior, raising significant ethical and constitutional concerns. By targeting individuals based on probabilities rather than facts, these systems undermine the presumption of innocence and create a chilling effect on free expression.

The Role of FBI Infragard and Private Targeting Companies

The enforcement of blue and red lists involves a network of public and private entities, with the FBI's Infragard program and private targeting companies playing central roles. Infragard is an initiative led by the FBI that connects the federal government with private-sector partners to protect critical infrastructure ostensibly. However, whistleblowers have revealed that Infragard also facilitates targeting individuals flagged as threats. By leveraging its extensive network of corporate partners, Infragard coordinates surveillance and harassment campaigns, often operating beyond the reach of public accountability.

Private targeting companies are contracted to conduct surveillance and harass individuals on the red list. These firms monitor their targets using advanced technologies such as geolocation tracking, facial recognition, and AI-driven analytics. They also employ psychological tactics, including spreading disinformation and sabotaging relationships, to isolate and destabilize these individuals. These operations often blur the line between government actions and corporate overreach, creating a shadow system of enforcement that operates with minimal oversight.

Gangstalking and Organized Harassment

One of the most disturbing aspects of the blue and red lists is the use of gangstalking tactics to intimidate and harass individuals on the red list. Gangstalking involves coordinated efforts by multiple actors to monitor, disrupt, and psychologically torment a target. These campaigns are designed to create a sense of paranoia and helplessness, ultimately silencing dissent and breaking the target's resolve.

Targets of gangstalking report being followed in public, monitored in their homes and subjected to subtle but persistent harassment. This can include everything from strange phone calls to unexplained damage to personal property. Social sabotage is another common tactic, with false rumors spread to damage the target's reputation and relationships. Advanced surveillance technology, including drones and hidden cameras, makes these campaigns even more invasive. While gangstalking is often dismissed as paranoia, accounts from whistleblowers and victims suggest that it is a natural and systematic practice tied to the broader framework of citizen labeling and control.

The CDC's Role in Detention

The Centers for Disease Control and Prevention (CDC) plays a critical role in the system of control enabled by the blue and red lists. Under the Public Health Service Act, the CDC can isolate or quarantine individuals deemed threats to public health. While this power is ostensibly designed to contain infectious diseases, it raises significant concerns about potential misuse.

During the COVID-19 pandemic, the CDC expanded its quarantine protocols, creating a legal framework for the detention of individuals flagged as risks. Critics warn that these powers could be used to target red-list individuals under the pretense of public health. By framing dissent or noncompliance as a medical threat, the government gains a powerful tool for suppressing opposition without invoking traditional legal processes. This integration of public health measures with surveillance and targeting systems represents a dangerous convergence of authority.

The Military's Role and the Erosion of Posse Comitatus

The Department of Defense's (DoD) recent directive authorizing the military to use lethal force against Americans in specific scenarios further escalates the risks posed by the blue and red lists. This directive, which some argue violates the Posse Comitatus Act, aligns military enforcement with existing surveillance and targeting systems. Red-list individuals could be identified and targeted for military action during a declared emergency, further blurring the line between military and civilian authority. This development represents a chilling expansion of militarized governance, raising serious questions about the future of constitutional protections.

A System of Control

The blue and red lists and the organizations and tactics used to enforce them create a comprehensive system for managing dissent and ensuring compliance. The government has established a framework prioritizing control over freedom by categorizing citizens, suppressing dissent, and utilizing agencies like the FBI, CDC, and DoD. While presented as necessary for national security, this system undermines the principles of democracy and equality.Awareness and resistance are crucial to challenging these systems. By exposing their existence and demanding transparency, citizens can combat the erosion of their rights. The struggle against these lists is not solely about protecting individual freedoms; it is about defending the very essence of democracy. This chapter emphasizes the urgent need to resist the normalization of such systems before they become ingrained in everyday life.

Chapter 21

Return of the Anunnaki: Watching, Waiting, Judging

The legacy of the Anunnaki, shrouded in mystery, has captivated scholars, scientists, and truth-seekers for decades. According to the ancient Sumerians, these powerful beings descended to Earth from Nibiru, a planet within the Nemesis star system. Revered as gods, the Anunnaki were believed to have created humanity to mine Earth's resources, particularly gold, and left profound prophecies about their eventual return. The Sumerians believed that the Anunnaki's reappearance would coincide with cosmic disturbances, societal upheaval, and moments of judgment for humanity.

In recent years, events that defy conventional explanations have fueled speculation about Anunnaki's return. Unexplained lights above the White House and rumored sightings of a ten-foot alien at a Miami mall have added new layers to the mystery. Combined with increasing signs of celestial disturbances from the Nemesis star system, these phenomena could suggest that the Anunnaki are closer than we realize. Are they watching humanity from afar, waiting to intervene? Or are they already among us, observing and preparing for the next chapter of their interaction with Earth? This chapter explores the history, mythology, and modern evidence that point toward a potential reckoning with these ancient watchers, sparking curiosity about the potential implications of their return.

The Sumerian Legacy and Anunnaki Prophecies

The Sumerians are often called the cradle of civilization, having established a complex society over 5,000 years ago with advanced knowledge in mathematics, astronomy, and agriculture. Among their most significant contributions are their mythological texts, which detail the accounts of the Anunnaki. These beings were described not as abstract deities but as physical entities who came to Earth in search of resources. According to the *Enuma Elish* and other Sumerian writings, the Anunnaki originated from Nibiru, a planet with an elliptical orbit that periodically brings it close to Earth.

The texts portray Nibiru as part of the Nemesis star system, a celestial configuration that causes chaos when it passes through our solar system. The Anunnaki were said to have created humanity through genetic engineering, merging their DNA with that of early hominids to develop a workforce capable of extracting Earth's resources. Gold was particularly valued, as the Anunnaki used it to stabilize their planet's atmosphere by dispersing fine gold particles into the stratosphere—an ancient precursor to modern geo-engineering techniques.

Although the Anunnaki eventually departed from Earth, Sumerian prophecies predicted their return. According to these texts, this return would coincide with Nibiru's following close passage, heralding a time of cosmic disturbances and judgment. The Anunnaki would return to observe humanity, assess its actions, and determine its fate. Once dismissed as mere mythology, these stories now resonate with contemporary astronomical discoveries and global events, suggesting they may contain deeper truths.

Modern Astronomical Evidence

In 1983, NASA's Infrared Astronomical Satellite (IRAS) detected what appeared to be a large, distant object beyond Pluto. Initial speculation focused on the possibility of a massive planet or a failed star, later known as "Planet X" or "Nemesis." While mainstream scientists were cautious in their interpretations, independent researchers argued that this discovery supported ancient accounts of Nibiru and the Nemesis star system.

In the following decades, further evidence emerged as astronomers observed anomalies in the orbits of trans-Neptune objects. These anomalies suggested the gravitational influence of a hidden celestial body. Theoretical models describe this object as a massive planet or a brown dwarf with an elongated orbit, aligning with Nibiru's descriptions. Its periodic approach could explain the cyclical cataclysms recorded in ancient texts, including floods, earthquakes, and volcanic eruptions.

If this theory is accurate, the approach of the Nemesis star system could have profound implications for Earth. The gravitational pull of such a massive body could disrupt Earth's tectonic stability, potentially triggering natural disasters on an unprecedented scale. This idea corresponds with the Sumerian accounts of chaos preceding the return of the Anunnaki. If these disruptions are already occurring, as some researchers claim, then Nibiru's presence in our solar system may be closer than we think.

Recent Sightings – Signs of Their Return?

In January 2024, mysterious lights appeared above the White House, igniting a wave of speculation. Witnesses described orb-like objects emitting pulsating lights, hovering in formation before vanishing without a trace. Videos of the event quickly went viral, prompting debates about their origin. While government officials downplayed the incident, attributing it to drones or atmospheric anomalies, the unusual characteristics of the lights led many to believe they were extraterrestrial.

Just days earlier, reports of a ten-foot alien sighting threw a Miami mall into chaos. Witnesses described the figure as humanoid but distinctly otherworldly, with glowing eyes and an unearthly gait. Although skeptics dismissed the incident as a hoax, the sheer number of eyewitnesses and the panic it caused suggest something extraordinary occurred. Grainy footage shows a tall, luminous figure moving through the mall before disappearing.

These sightings, coupled with the increasing frequency of UFO reports worldwide, have led to speculation that the Anunnaki may already be observing humanity. Ancient texts describe their habit of making their presence known through subtle yet unmistakable signs, such as unexplained lights or the appearance of otherworldly beings. If these incidents are connected, they could signify the beginning of the Anunnaki's re-engagement with Earth.

The Judgment of Humanity

The Sumerians depicted the Anunnaki as creators and judges, possessing the capacity for great kindness and harsh retribution. Ancient texts suggest that their judgment is not arbitrary but based on humanity's adherence to cosmic principles of balance and stewardship. The return of the Anunnaki would signal a moment of reckoning, during which humanity's actions would be evaluated and its fate determined, creating a sense of anticipation and apprehension among the audience.

Modern humanity presents a complex picture. While technological advancements have brought remarkable progress, they have also led to widespread environmental destruction, social inequality, and moral decline. The relentless pursuit of profit and power, often at the expense of ethical considerations, raises questions about how humanity would fare under the Anunnaki's scrutiny.

If the Anunnaki's return is imminent, their judgment could manifest in various ways. They might guide humanity through challenges by offering knowledge and technology to address pressing issues. Alternatively, they could impose corrective measures, disrupting systems that have strayed too far from their intended purpose. The outcome would depend on the Anunnaki's intentions and humanity's willingness to change.

Geopolitical Movements and Anunnaki Artifacts

The U.S. military's actions in Iraq during the early 2000s have long been a source of intrigue. Among the sites targeted in these operations were ancient ruins and artifacts tied to the Sumerians, including cylinder seals and tablets containing detailed accounts of the Anunnaki. Some researchers believe these artifacts hold critical information about communicating with or preparing for Anunnaki's return.

In addition to archaeological efforts, governments worldwide have invested heavily in underground facilities, advanced space programs, and disaster preparedness initiatives. These measures suggest that global powers are aware of an impending event, whether it be the Nemesis star system's approach or the Anunnaki's return. The secrecy surrounding these efforts raises questions about what information is being withheld from the public and why.

Are the Anunnaki Already Among Us?

One of the most provocative theories is that the Anunnaki never left but have remained on Earth, observing and influencing humanity from behind the scenes. Ancient texts describe their ability to disguise themselves and interact with humans without revealing their true nature. The Miami mall sighting and other reports of humanoid figures with unusual characteristics echo these accounts, suggesting that the Anunnaki may already be preparing for a more overt return.

The increase in UFO sightings and unexplained phenomena further supports this theory. If the Anunnaki are watching, these incidents could represent reconnaissance missions or early attempts to gauge humanity's readiness. Their actions, as described in Sumerian texts, have always been deliberate and strategic, choosing moments of great significance to intervene.

The Dawn of a New Epoch

If true, the return of the Anunnaki would mark a significant turning point in human history. It would challenge our understanding of science, religion, and the origins of civilization, forcing humanity to confront profound questions about its place in the cosmos. Recent events, including astronomical anomalies and mysterious sightings, suggest that ancient prophecies may unfold before our eyes.

As Earth grapples with environmental, social, and geopolitical crises, the possibility of extraterrestrial judgment adds an unsettling dimension to our challenges. The Anunnaki's return could reveal humanity's past and shape its future. Whether they arrive as saviors, judges, or something in between, their presence would reshape the world in ways we can scarcely imagine.

Chapter 22

When Worlds Collide: The Final Perihelion and Global Fallout

Humanity has encountered catastrophic events that fundamentally reshaped civilizations, ecosystems, and the planet. These disasters—from ancient floods to mass extinctions—have profoundly influenced our collective experience. However, these events are not merely random occurrences but part of a grand cosmic cycle driven by forces beyond Earth. Ancient prophecies and modern scientific observations converge on a powerful truth: the periodic return of the Nemesis star system represents a celestial threat that could unleash unimaginable destruction.

As the Nemesis system, dominated by the enigmatic Planet X (Nibiru), approaches its final perihelion with Earth, humanity stands at the precipice of a new epoch. The upheavals instigated by this celestial intruder will push Earth's natural systems to their breaking point. Catastrophic events, including 400-mph winds, supervolcanic eruptions, asteroid impacts, and widespread liquefaction, are poised to strike unprecedentedly. Humanity's only refuge may lie underground, but the inevitable societal collapse preceding these disasters will render billions vulnerable to chaos. This chapter decisively examines the mechanics of Nibiru's final approach, the extreme disasters it will unleash, and the breakdown of society as we face an impending apocalypse.

The Mechanics of Nibiru's Orbit

The Nemesis star system is theorized to be a burnt-out brown dwarf star accompanied by several orbiting planets. It follows an elongated, elliptical orbit that periodically intersects our solar system. Among its celestial companions, Nibiru stands out as a massive and dense planet with a gravitational pull strong enough to disrupt the orbits of other planets. Every 3,600 years, this system reaches its perihelion—the point in its orbit closest to the Sun—bringing it dangerously close to Earth.

During its approach, Nibiru's gravitational and electromagnetic forces can destabilize Earth's delicate balance. These forces may disrupt tectonic plates, cause Earth's magnetic field shifts, and even influence atmospheric systems. Historical records, including Sumerian texts and biblical accounts, vividly describe these disruptions, suggesting that previous Nibiru passages have left a devastation trail.

Modern scientific observations lend some credibility to these ancient accounts. Anomalies in the orbits of trans-Neptunian objects, unexplained shifts in planetary alignments, and reports of celestial objects entering our solar system all point to the existence of a massive, unseen force. While mainstream astronomers remain cautious, independent researchers argue that Nibiru's evidence is mounting and its effects may already be felt.

The Prelude to Catastrophe

Signs of Nibiru's approach have accumulated for years, manifesting as an increase in extreme weather events, seismic activity, and environmental anomalies. Biblical-level flooding has become a recurring headline, with entire regions submerged under rising waters. Southeast Asia, parts of Europe, and coastal cities in North America have experienced unprecedented inundation, forcing millions to flee their homes. Yet, mainstream media remains largely silent on the global scale of these disasters, choosing instead to downplay their significance.

Volcanic activity has also surged, with dormant giants showing signs of awakening. Yellowstone National Park, home to one of the world's most dangerous supervolcanoes, has experienced increased seismic swarms and ground deformation. If Yellowstone were to erupt, the resulting ash cloud would plunge the world into a volcanic winter, blocking sunlight and collapsing agricultural systems.

Asteroid threats have similarly escalated, with NASA identifying numerous near-Earth objects on collision courses during the pandemic years. Apophis, an asteroid expected to make a close approach in 2029, looms as a potential harbinger of destruction. Some researchers suggest that Nibiru's gravitational influence dislodges celestial debris, sending it hurtling toward Earth in a deadly cascade.

The Peak of the Event – When Worlds Collide

At the height of Nibiru's passage, Earth will face a series of severe cascading disasters that are so severe that survival on the surface will become nearly impossible. Among the most terrifying phenomena will be unrelenting 400-mph straight-line winds generated by the destabilization of jet streams and atmospheric currents. These winds shred buildings, uproot trees, and turn debris into lethal projectiles. No structure, no matter how reinforced, will be safe from the fury of these storms.

Simultaneously, Earth's tectonic plates will buckle under the strain of Nibiru's gravitational pull, triggering supervolcanic eruptions. Yellowstone and other massive calderas around the globe will erupt with catastrophic force, ejecting billions of tons of ash and gases into the atmosphere. The resulting volcanic winter could last years, plunging temperatures and decimating crops worldwide.

Fueled by celestial debris drawn from the Nemesis system, asteroid impact will add another layer of destruction. These impacts will cause regional annihilation, creating shockwaves, firestorms, and tsunamis hundreds of feet high. Coastal cities like New York, Tokyo, and Mumbai will be erased from the map, while island nations will disappear entirely beneath the waves.

Perhaps the most insidious effect will be the induction heating of Earth's crust caused by electromagnetic disturbances from Nibiru. This process will liquefy vast swaths of land, rendering entire regions unstable. Buildings, roads, and infrastructure will sink into the ground as the very foundation of the Earth dissolves. Earthquakes of unimaginable magnitude will become a daily occurrence, fracturing continents and reshaping coastlines.

Living Underground – Humanity's Last Refuge

Faced with extreme conditions, humanity's only chance for survival will lie underground. Underground bunkers, long prepared by governments and the wealthy elite, will become the last bastions of human life. These facilities, equipped with advanced life-support systems, hydroponic farms, and stockpiles of resources, are designed to sustain life for years or even decades.

However, access to these bunkers will be restricted to a select few—government officials, scientists, military personnel, and the ultra-wealthy. For the rest of humanity, the surface will become a living hell. Those who manage to survive the initial onslaught of disasters will face starvation, disease, and violence in a world stripped of its resources.

Life underground will also be fraught with challenges. The lack of sunlight and fresh air will damage physical and mental health, while the confined spaces will exacerbate social tensions. Communities must adapt to artificial environments, relying on strict resource management and cooperation to endure long periods of isolation. Yet, amidst the disasters raging above, the underground will remain humanity's only refuge.

The Collapse of Society

Before Nibiru becomes visible in the sky, society will already be unraveling. As news spreads of the approaching catastrophe, panic will take hold. Economic systems will collapse as people abandon jobs, hoard supplies, and withdraw from societal norms. Governments will impose martial law to maintain order, but these efforts will only delay the inevitable.

Once Nibiru becomes visible, its presence will trigger widespread hysteria. Seeing a massive celestial body looming in the sky will confirm the worst fears and send shockwaves through every corner of society. Religious movements will proclaim the end times while scientists and governments scramble to address the fallout. Supply chains will disintegrate, leaving billions without access to food, water, or medical care. Violence will erupt as people fight for dwindling resources, and cities will become war zones.

Returning to their underground bunkers, the elite will abandon the surface world to its fate. For those left behind, survival will depend on sheer luck and ingenuity. By the time Nibiru reaches its closest point to Earth, society as we know it will have ceased to exist.

Aftermath – A New World

When the Nemesis system finally departs, Earth will be forever changed. New continents and coastlines will emerge from the chaos, while old ones will vanish beneath the waves. The survivors, whether underground or on the surface, will face the monumental task of rebuilding civilization from the ruins.

The atmosphere, filled with ash and debris, will be hostile to life. Crops will struggle to grow in poisoned soil, and clean water will be a rare commodity. Survivors will have to deal not only with the aftermath of natural disasters but also with the psychological scars left by their ordeal.

Yet, amidst the destruction, there will be hope. The survivors, hardened by their experiences, will have the opportunity to build a new world—one informed by past mistakes and guided by the resilience of the human spirit. Whether they rise to this occasion or fall into the same patterns of greed and division remains to be seen.

Cosmic Chaos

The final perihelion of the Nemesis star system represents humanity's ultimate test. As forces beyond its control reshape Earth, survival will depend on adaptability, resilience, and unity. The disasters we face are not random but part of a larger cosmic cycle that challenges humanity to confront its vulnerabilities and rise above them.

Chapter 23

The Final Chapter: Rise or Fall?

The Nemesis star system has receded, leaving Earth irrevocably changed. Cities have crumbled, coastlines have vanished, and survivors face a daunting reality: rebuilding a world where the scars of cosmic upheaval are visible in every landscape. This catastrophic period, foretold by ancient texts and partially revealed through modern science, has tested humanity's resilience, resourcefulness, and morality, showcasing the indomitable spirit of the human race.

Standing on the brink of a new era, we must ask ourselves: Will we rise from the ashes, wiser and more united, to create a sustainable future? Or will we succumb to chaos and division, leading to the final collapse of our civilization?

This chapter explores the choices before us as humanity reaches a critical juncture—a crossroads in time that will define the fate of our species for millennia. It is a moment of both reckoning and profound opportunity.

A World Transformed

In the aftermath of the Nemesis system's passage, Earth has become unrecognizable. Massive tectonic upheavals have shifted continents, and new coastlines have emerged from the wreckage of tsunamis and flooding. Cities like New York, Tokyo, and Mumbai have vanished beneath the ocean, their skylines replaced by vast stretches of water. Mountain ranges have crumbled or risen anew, while once-fertile plains have transformed into deserts or swamps.

The atmosphere, thick with volcanic ash and debris, has plunged the planet into a prolonged winter. Sunlight struggles to penetrate the dense cloud cover, leaving Earth shrouded in a twilight haze. Crops have failed, ecosystems are in disarray, and species that once thrived now teeter on the brink of extinction. Survivors must adapt to a harsh new reality, where the comforts of the old world have given way to a primal struggle for survival.

The infrastructure that supported modern society lies in ruins. Power grids, communication networks, and transportation systems have been obliterated. The scattered and desperate survivors face the monumental task of rebuilding, aware that the resources and knowledge they once took for granted are now rare luxuries.

The Survivors – Divided or United?

The survivors of the catastrophe are divided into two primary groups: those who endured the destruction on the surface and those who retreated to underground bunkers. Each group has its strengths, weaknesses, and challenges, shaped by vastly different experiences.

Surface survivors have developed resilience, resourcefulness, and an intimate knowledge of the transformed environment. They are battle-hardened and deeply connected to the land, but they lack the technological advantages and resources of the bunker dwellers. On the other hand, the bunker communities emerge with stockpiles of supplies and advanced technologies but face the psychological toll of isolation and disconnection from the surface world.

The potential for conflict between these groups is high, mainly as they compete for resources and leadership. However, the power of cooperation offers a more promising path. If surface survivors and bunker dwellers can unite their strengths, combining practical skills with advanced tools, they can create a foundation for rebuilding civilization. The choice between division and unity will be one of the defining factors in humanity's future, emphasizing the importance of coming together in times of crisis.

Ancient Knowledge and Modern Challenges

The survivors' greatest asset may lie in the wisdom of the past. The Sumerian texts, long dismissed as mythology, have proven prophetic in their descriptions of cosmic cycles and catastrophic events. These ancient records and artifacts recovered from archaeological sites could hold the keys to understanding the challenges ahead, sparking a renewed interest in ancient knowledge and its relevance in the modern world.

Technologies and philosophies attributed to the Anunnaki may offer solutions to humanity's most pressing problems. Advanced engineering techniques, energy systems, and methods for sustainable living could be rediscovered, providing a roadmap for recovery. However, the dissemination of this knowledge will be critical. If hoarded by elites, it could widen the gap between factions and create new forms of oppression. It could become a unifying force if shared equitably, guiding humanity toward a brighter future.

Spiritual and religious traditions will also play a significant role in rebuilding. For many, the events of the Nemesis passage confirm the validity of ancient prophecies, reinforcing their faith and providing a sense of purpose. Others may see this as an opportunity to transcend divisive ideologies and embrace a more universal understanding of humanity's place in the cosmos. Balancing these perspectives will be essential to fostering harmony in a fractured world.

A New Relationship with Technology

Ancient and modern technology will be essential for humanity's recovery. Survivors need to prioritize resilient, adaptable, and sustainable systems. The centralized, fragile networks of the old world must be replaced with decentralized, community-driven solutions that empower individuals and promote self-sufficiency.

The rediscovery of Anunnaki technologies could revolutionize the rebuilding process. If used responsibly, these advancements could provide clean energy, efficient food production, and innovative ways to adapt to the Earth's changed environment. However, the potential for misuse of technology remains a significant risk. While valuable tools, artificial intelligence, robotics, and automation could also become instruments of oppression if controlled by authoritarian groups.

A new ethical framework is necessary to ensure that technology serves humanity rather than dominates it. Survivors must balance innovation with caution, utilizing their tools to heal the planet and uplift society rather than repeating past mistakes.

The Struggle for Resources

In the post-cataclysmic world, resources will be the currency of survival. Freshwater, arable land, and energy sources will become the most valuable commodities, and their scarcity will drive conflict and cooperation.

Communities prioritizing sustainable practices, such as aquaponics, renewable energy, and resource sharing, will thrive best. These localized systems can create resilient networks capable of weathering future challenges. However, centralized control of resources by powerful factions could lead to exploitation and inequality, undermining efforts to build a fair and stable society.

The redistribution of resources will also challenge traditional notions of wealth and power. In a world where survival depends on collaboration, resource hoarding will be both impractical and unacceptable. A new social contract, grounded in equity and mutual aid, will be essential to fostering long-term stability.

A Crossroads in Time

As the dust settles and the survivors take their first steps into the new era, humanity is at a crossroads. The choices made at this moment will shape the trajectory of civilization for millennia. Will we learn from the mistakes that led to our near-destruction, embracing cooperation, sustainability, and a deeper connection to the Earth? Or will we repeat the greed, division, and exploitation cycles that have often defined our history?

This is not merely a question of survival but of identity. The trials of the Nemesis passage have revealed humanity's potential for greatness and destruction. The challenge now is to harness that potential for the greater good, creating a society that values balance, justice, and the pursuit of knowledge.

At this crossroads, the future remains uncertain. The cosmic forces that have reshaped our planet remind us of our fragility and resilience. They challenge us to rise above our limitations and forge a new path that honors the lessons of the past while embracing the possibilities of the future.

Rise or Fall?

The final chapter of humanity's story has yet to be written. The passage of the Nemesis star system marks the end of one era and the beginning of another, presenting us with both immense challenges and profound opportunities. The question is simple yet significant: Will we rise to the occasion and create a new world grounded in unity and sustainability? Or will we succumb to chaos, ensuring that the mistakes of the past become the legacy of the future?

This moment is a reckoning and a choice. It represents a crossroads in time where our decisions will resonate across the millennia. Let us choose wisely, for the stakes could not be higher.

About the Author

Shepard Ambellas, a pioneering investigative journalist, author, and filmmaker, is renowned for his courage in uncovering stories that challenge mainstream narratives and unveil the hidden forces shaping our world. With decades of experience exposing government cover-ups, clandestine operations, and the intersection of politics, science, and spirituality, Ambellas has established himself as a fearless truth-seeker and a prominent voice in alternative media.

His influence extends globally, having appeared on significant platforms such as the Travel Channel's *America Declassified*, the legendary radio show *Coast to Coast AM with George Noory*, and *The Alex Jones Show*, including in-studio appearances with Alex Jones. His work has been featured on the Drudge Report, Infowars, and other influential outlets, sparking meaningful conversations about pressing issues and reaching audiences worldwide.

As the founder and editor-in-chief of *Intellihub News and Politics* (now Sqauk.com), Ambellas has authored over 6,000 reports, unveiling groundbreaking stories about global events, deep state operations, and alternative perspectives often overlooked by corporate media. His fearless approach to journalism has made him a trusted source for those seeking answers to the world's most significant and controversial questions.

Ambellas is also the creator of the critically acclaimed feature documentary *Shackled to Silence*, which explores the hidden agendas behind global crises, including the COVID-19 pandemic, and how these events are linked to broader plans for societal control. His investigative work ties historical truths to modern conspiracies, offering readers and viewers a compelling lens through which to understand the world.

In *Hidden Axis: Forces Beyond the Visible World*, Ambellas draws upon years of research, insider information, and his deep understanding of ancient texts to connect the dots between the past, present, and future. By combining investigative journalism with captivating storytelling, he takes readers on a journey through cosmic forces, deep state agendas, and apocalyptic scenarios threatening humanity's existence—and the choices we must make to shape our destiny.

Ambellas's unwavering commitment to truth is a cornerstone of his work. He continues to challenge the status quo and illuminate the unseen forces at work in our world, inspiring others to question the world around them. When he is not writing or investigating, Ambellas enjoys exploring nature and experimenting with survival techniques.

Links and Merch

I would greatly appreciate your support! You can find all my links and merchandise conveniently on my Linktree. Just scan the QR code to explore. Thank you!

Shepard Ambellas